Models of Procurement & Supply Chain Management

Paul Jackson,
Barry Crocker
& Ray Carter

Cambridge
Academic

ISBN 1-903-499-87-9
978-1-903499-87-0

Printed and bound in the United Kingdom by 4edge Ltd, 7a Eldon Way Industrial Estate, Hockley, Essex, SS5 4AD.

CONTENTS

INTRODUCTION

The concept of Procurement and Supply Chain Management is now a well-recognised and defined profession with established processes and infrastructure. Its cross-functional contribution and its need to engage stakeholders from both within and outside the organisation makes it core to the development of strategy and delivery of successful outcomes throughout.

As an industry, the development of models, tools and processes to help illustrate opportunities, drive analysis, dissect problems and generate strategic philosophy is fundamental to its success, with the overall objective of reducing cost whilst improving quality, effectiveness and efficiency. Utilising some of these philosophies within a culture embracing continuous improvement and vision is essential.

Over the years the extent and breadth of the contribution of the Procurement and Supply Chain Management function to the operation of the organisation has become more visible and better publicised. This has inevitably led to increased investment in training and development and has led to a rise in organisations supporting and underpinning the industry, organisations such as CIPS, IACCM, IIAPS, ISM, IFPSM, PASIA and a host of other international and regional institutions.

All the main Procurement and Supply Chain institutions incorporate structure and mechanism to enable the training and development of its members with qualifications, examinations and CPD (Continuous Profession Development) activities at its core. These development constructs utilise many of the popular business models, yet few publications are readily available to succinctly collate these models in a user-friendly yet affordable manner.

And remember, in exams "Models Mean Marks".

And therein lies the motivation and challenge embraced by the authors; our intention with this publication is therefore summarised as follows:

1. To collate the most common, popular and effective Procurement and Supply Chain models into one publication;
2. To remain succinct in the definition, explanation and critique of each model;

3. To remain affordable, concise and user-friendly both to students and practitioners.

WHAT EXACTLY DOES THE BOOK CONTAIN?

In short, this publication contains a 101 diverse and cross-functional models which the authors and some of their esteemed colleagues deem to be of greatest value, and which they have found to be of most use when working within global organisations, delivering consultancy activities or teaching Procurement and Supply Chain subjects to international students studying CIPS and other qualifications.

Each model or tool is contained within a single page, headed with a short definition, followed by further detail and explanation, analysis of any evolutions and iterations, with an "advantages and disadvantages" critique to conclude. A summary web or phone app will then support these pages in due course with a keyword driven solution enabling the user to identify models most appropriate to their issue or activity. A Twitter feed also supports the sentiment of the book, see @Models of Business, and acts as a reminder to students and users of the importance of models within their chosen field.

Further, as a supplementary feature, some nominal direction is given as to where the models may fit into the procurement or operational process, where they might deliver value to the organisation, or where they may be used to develop corporate strategy.

WHO IS THIS BOOK FOR?

A fundamental question for any aspiring author is "who will read my book?" Clearly, without a defined understanding of "the who", a text can become distracted and lose sight of its fundamental objectives.

In short, therefore, this book is intended for all of the following readership groups:

*   **Students** studying for Procurement, Supply Chain, Logistics, general business, management, sales, and other related courses or examinations.
*   **Organisational users** looking to improve operational or commercial performance by using internationally recognised models proven to increase

efficiency, raise awareness of issues, reduce waste, exploit opportunities, manage risk, and so on.
- **Management** looking to evaluate performance, exploit external opportunities and generate strategy to deliver the corporate vision.
- **Sales personnel** and anybody else with a corporate interest in evaluating the actions of others with a view to determining their strategic ambitions.

AND WHY WRITE THIS BOOK?

During our teaching and consultancy work over the years, we have seen the use and application of many Procurement, Supply Chain and management models. These models help the user understand, evaluate or position features and characteristics to enable a more considered assessment and diagnosis throughout the Procurement process.

The structure of the Procurement process (See figure 1) may differ from organisation to organisation or within different jurisdictions, however the fundamental chain of events is fairly standard with the same overall objective of securing some form of goods or services to fulfil the user requirements, in a compliant, fair and equitable manner, whilst recognising the Five Rights, and ensuring best use of corporate resources. The Procurement process should however be clearly defined, consistent and users trained in its operation, and will need input and assessments throughout its operation, incorporating many of the models contained within this book.

Over the years, some models have become widely understood and used – for example the SWOT analysis to assess the internal features of an organisation, project, team, etc – whilst others have evolved as the needs of the user have changed – for example PEST, became PESTLE, became STEEPLE, and now STEEPLED.

For the user, understanding the portfolio of models – as well as any iterations that have evolved – is critical if the corporate resource is to be used to full effect. Many models have blurred edges or vagaries in their objectives, whilst others are arguably just mutations or reinventions of other similar models.

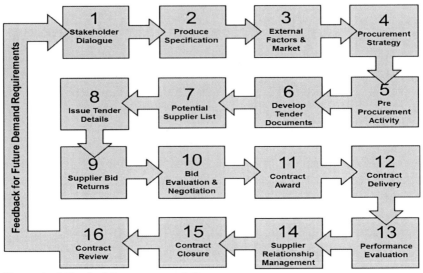

Figure 1: A Typical Procurement Process

Within this sea of models there are, however, some models which are fundamental to the success of an organisation or protagonists therein. Many of these – for example Porter's Five Forces in the evaluation of a market – have been instrumental in developing how aspects are viewed and appraised. Such models, whilst commonly recognised and appreciated, formed the initial foundations of this work, created in the first instance to assist students in Nigeria understand the models that could be used within international Procurement, Supply Chain, and management examinations to help develop answers and gain extra marks.

Some considerable dialogue and deliberation was also undertaken as to the depth and extent that each model should reflect. Whilst there are other similar publications available over a greater depth of a few main models, our intention here is to provide a broad range of models with each review providing a succinct assessment of that model in a form that is both easy to absorb and retain on the part of the reader, whilst contained in length to ensure affordability recognising that for many this book should form an examination guide or *aide memoire*. In addition, to complement this publication, a short-form web-app has been generated to give a very high level overview of each model based on a keyword search mechanism, and the aforementioned Twitter feed helps reiterate the need to use models in exams and highlights their relevance to business process and strategy.

Whilst each Procurement and Supply Chain institution has its own anomalies within its syllabus, the content of this book, by its very nature applies equally across all. There is therefore no singularity of focus on any one syllabus or institution, nor is it intended that the content is necessarily restricted to these aforementioned groups. There are, however, some generic thoughts as to how models could be used to explore and develop exam answers, with many marking schemes having an allocation of marks to reward such usage, especially where the purpose of the assessment is to assess the diagnostic skills of the student against a specific case study or market scenario.

In conclusion therefore, this work reflects a clear need identified over many years of consultancy and teaching. We intend this text to be an affordable production full of common and popular models to help the user and student improve their lot.

Section 1 // Business Relationships

- Burnes & New Customer/Supplier Relationships
- Cox Supplier Relationships Management Model
- Crocker Managing Satisfaction of Service Quality Model
- Customer-Supplier Partnership Bridge
- Purchaser-Supplier Satisfaction Model
- Relationship Determination Model
- Supplier Relationship Management (SRM) Interfaces
- Watson & Sanderson Buyer-Supplier Power Model

1. BURNES & NEW CUSTOMER/SUPPLIER RELATIONSHIPS

The Burnes & New Customer/Supplier Relationships Model examines the issue of cost and benefit secured by the buyer and the supplier in collaborative approaches within Procurement and Supply Chain activities.

The Burnes & New Customer/Supplier Relationships Model depicts the contentious issue of imbalances between the distribution of costs and benefits from a collaborative approach. Evidence suggests that the benefits appear easier to achieve than is often the case. The research which underpins the model highlights the imbalance in the costs and benefits of various initiatives, shown below:

Customer/Supplier Relationships

New.S, Burnes.B (1998) Developing effective customer supply relationships IJQRM [1]

Burnes & New suggest that a win-lose outcome is often masked by an aura of collaboration, with some findings showing a predominance of costs borne by the supplier (rather than shared) with the costs perhaps perceived as an investment by the supplier to secure longer term benefits. The implication of the model is that there appears to be a need for more of a *"trust with verification approach"*. This model does not validate the concept of win-win, but does indicate that a more sophisticated, longer-term view of the relative costs and benefits of collaboration may need to be taken.

Positive Views on Model	Negative Views on Model
• Supported with detailed research	• Complicated and arguably very subjective

2. COX SUPPLIER RELATIONSHIPS MANAGEMENT MODEL

The Cox Supplier Relationships Management Model looks at the Buyer-supplier relationships which are characterised by two main elements: the nature of the interaction between the two parties and the manner in which the benefits of the relationship are divided between the two parties

The two dimensions (Relationship Type and Sharing of Gain) provide four generic relationship types rejecting the idea that buyer-supplier relationships adhere to neat contrasts e.g. Arm's Length and Collaborative Interactions. For instance, Adversarial Collaborative (such as between a large retailer and small supplier) doesn't provide a win-win unless there is a niche being fulfilled.

Power affects the expectation of the parties over the commercial returns that should accrue from the relationship and thus affects their willingness to invest in collaborative activities. The model assists managers make relationship decisions and frame their relationship expectations around their assessment of the costs and benefits in a particular type of interaction.

Working Methods

	Arm's Length	Close Collaborative
Unequal	**Adversarial Arm's Length**	**Adversarial Collaborative**
Equal	**Non-Adversarial Arm's Length**	**Non Adversarial Collaborative**

Sharing of Relationship Gain

Cox Supplier Relationship Types

This model was published in 'Improving Procurement & Supply Competence' in Lamming, R and Cox, A, (eds), *Strategic Procurement Management: Concepts & Cases* (!999) but further refined into a 9-box matrix in: Andrew Cox et al, *Business Relationships for Competitive Advantage* (2004).

Positive Views on Model	Negative Views on Model
• Strategises the relationship and brings the opportunity and value into the corporate context.	• Terminology and similar box labels can discourage use

3. CROCKER MANAGING SATISFACTION OF SERVICE QUALITY MODEL

The Crocker Managing Satisfaction of Service Quality Model combines levels of expectation and zone of tolerance, with (1) the outcome of a service, (2) level of satisfaction and (3) dissatisfaction.

Procurement must be fully attuned to its internal customers and understand their perceptions of a service in order to ensure that they fully appreciate what is, and what is not, acceptable in terms of service delivery.

It looks at how expectations give way to a perceived satisfaction using the service process. An example of a maintenance service can be applied to this model using data such as response time (e.g. one hour), arrival, diagnosis, actual time taken to fix on first attempt, discussion of findings, departure; and total elapsed time for the service. Performance within the zone of tolerance results in satisfaction, if the event occurs faster it may move into the higher zone and generate delight with the customer, or take longer leading to dissatisfaction.

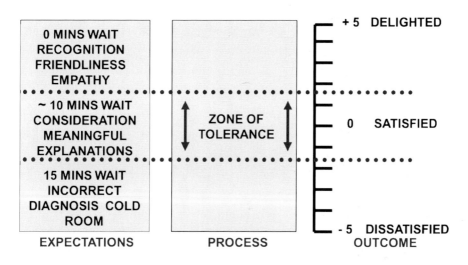

Positive Views on Model	Negative Views on Model
• Aligns the concepts of expectation and satisfaction with stakeholder tolerance	• Zone of tolerance and outcome can be very subjective

4. CUSTOMER-SUPPLIER PARTNERSHIP BRIDGE

The Customer-Supplier Partnership Bridge is used to identify and secure the benefits derivable from more collaborative, partnership style, supplier relationships and the establishment of trust.

The Customer-Supplier Partnership Bridge provides details of the key and foundational elements necessary for achieving effective customer–supplier relationships and delivery of mutual "win-win" benefits.

Trust can be defined as "one party's belief that the other party in the relationship will not knowingly exploit its vulnerabilities with adverse opportunistic behaviours, even when such exploitation would not be detected."

Customer Supplier Partnership Bridge

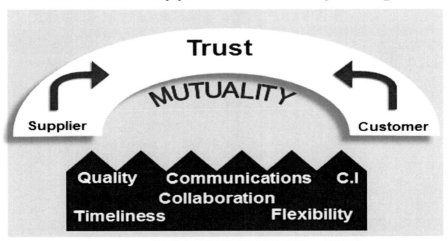

Both sides of the relationship are required to adapt their behaviours in order to ensure that these elements are capitalised upon. A major prerequisite for the model to succeed is Continuous Improvement (CI).

Positive Views on Model	Negative Views on Model
• Clear illustrative model • Illustrates the primary issues that need to come together to generate trust in a relationship	• Culture, risk and value may also need to be considered when developing trust and mutuality • Other diverse stakeholder engagement is recommended

5. PURCHASER-SUPPLIER SATISFACTION MODEL

The Purchaser-Supplier Satisfaction Model assesses the health of a buyer-supplier relationship. The assessment is complex as both parties have differing perceptions of the benefits emanating from the relationship.

In procurement activities, the optimum situation is often a win-win with both parties having complete satisfaction, in the top right of the quadrant, 10 out of 10 on both axis.

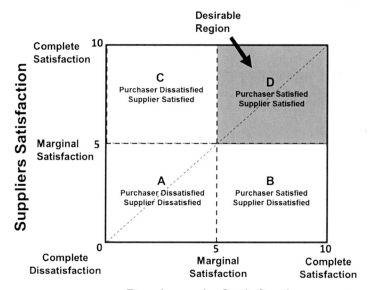

Clearly, the bottom left quadrant is a concern as both parties are dissatisfied and will thus desire to change or terminate the relationship. Movements along the diagonal line indicate equal impact for both parties. Movements can be made by buyer-side and supplier-side "**crunch**" and "**stroking**" **tools,** such as failure to pay, deliver or share information and feedback. It is imperative that the health of the relationship is assessed regularly as behaviours change over time thus affecting assessment.

Positive Views on Model	Negative Views on Model
• Helps to categorise different states of relationships	• Use of crunch tools may harm long-term relationships. • Crunch may have more of a net impact than a stroke

6. Relationship Determination Model

The Relationship Determination Model maps a continuum of relationships dependent upon the level of commitment required, from Competitive Leverage with a minimum level of trust and commitment through to Strategic Alliance with high levels of trust and mutual commitment.

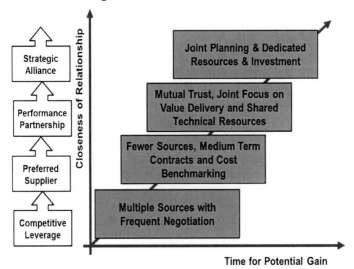

Competitive Leverage – a buyer's market with many suppliers and large client spend characterised by multiple sourcing, competitive tendering and frequent switching.

Preferred Suppliers are fewer in number and pre-qualified. For example, Toyota concentrates on structured supplier appraisal of Quality, Cost, Technical Expertise and Management Capability giving improved relationships, fewer defects, reduced cycle times and faster time to market.

Performance Partnership involves a small number of suppliers for co-development. Activities include: supplier rationalisation, joint CFTs, a focus on value, a reduction of Total Cost of Ownership and a high degree of Openness and Trust.

Strategic Alliances are very small in number and are associated with co-location and co-manufacturing. In order to move along the continuum there must be an appropriate distribution of gains i.e. a win-win relationship.

Positive Views on Model	Negative Views on Model
• Clearly categorises the different levels in buyer behaviour	• Doesn't consider risk or position of the supplier in the wider market

7. SUPPLIER RELATIONSHIP MANAGEMENT (SRM) INTERFACES

The Supplier Relationship Management (SRM) Interface model looks at how SRM and related Supply Chain functions are interrelated rather than linear and separate, as was traditionally the case. The procurement function generally owns the SRM governance model and processes, and facilitates the development of a cross-functional SRM capability.

Twice as many SRM leaders as followers (61%) have cross-functional teams assigned to strategic suppliers – an essential component in ensuring that relationships are managed in a consistent and co-ordinated way. Further, Leaders typically have full-time dedicated SRM managers in place for these relationships.

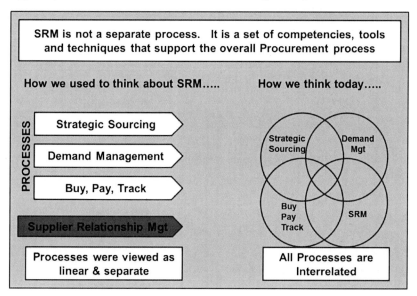

Leading organisations such as Proctor & Gamble invest heavily in training for these staff, with a focus on interpersonal skills such as communications, trust building, change management and cross-functional working.

Positive Views on Model	Negative Views on Model
• Recognised as being essential in terms of the successful implementation of SRM • Widely used in organisations	• Some users believe it is lacking in detail

8. WATSON & SANDERSON BUYER-SUPPLIER POWER MODEL

The Watson & Sanderson Buyer-Supplier Power Model looks at the different scenarios available in supply relationships as a result of a power balance/ imbalance generated as a result of the resources brought to the relationship by the Parties.

Although power advantages may rarely be explicitly exploited in interactions, the very existence of a power imbalance conditions buyer/supplier behaviour. The Watson & Sanderson model is constructed around four basic types of buyer/supplier behaviour power structure: buyer dominance, supplier dominance, buyer–supplier interdependence (high mutual dependence) and buyer–supplier dependence (low mutual dependence).

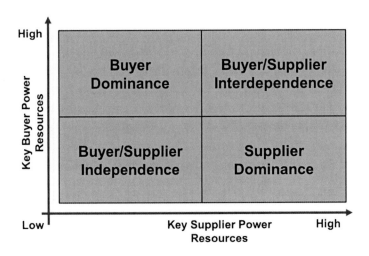

The fundamental premise is that the power of one party over another is determined by the extent to which that party is dependent on the other for resources (resource scarcity is impacted by high switching costs over an extended period). This assists the organisation in predicting the extent to which a firm would be able to effectively manage their supply relationships.

Positive Views on Model	Negative Views on Model
• Highlights dependency and interdependency	• Very simplistic and doesn't reflect competing powers

SECTION 2 // CONTRACT & PROJECT MANAGEMENT

- Carter 6S Contract Management Model
- Jackson SPARKLE Model
- Kotler 8 Phases of Change
- Lewin Freeze Model

9. CARTER 6S CONTRACT MANAGEMENT MODEL

The Carter 6S Contract Management Model is a robust six step contract management process, designed to ensure there is a clear statement of "what success looks like", show what makes a delighted customer and address how to manage and mitigate the risks associated with the project.

The Carter 6S Contract Management Model recognises the need for a clearly defined basis for the contract performance. It starts with ensuring that there is an unambiguous definition of what success would look like. The six steps are as follows:

Step 1 – **Success** – Supplier and Buyer need to define what is meant by success. Without having a clear idea of what is required and how it will be attained, failure is more likely to occur.

Step 2 – **Stakeholder Engagement** – Supplier and Buyer need to discuss and liaise with the Customer to ensure alignment of ideas or clear participation in the Supply Chain.

Step 3 – **Shared Vision** – Supplier and Buyer need to discuss the requirements and seek a clear and united vision of what is required.

Step 4 – **Specification** – Critical to success is that both Supplier and Buyer have an appropriate specification or scope of work to guide the contractors to ensure the output of goods or services meets Customer expectations.

Step 5 – **Strategy** – A robust, structured and coherent contracting strategy is required to make the contract come to life. For example, this strategy needs to consider cost, value, quality, CSR issues and risk.

Step 6 – **Suitable Contract** – Finally there is a need for the right type of contract, supported by a robust contract management system to guarantee as far as is possible, that output meets design and customer expectations.

Positive Views on Model	Negative Views on Model
• Model clearly addresses core issues in contract development • Model recognises the issues that cause problems in contract management	• Could look deeper at the evolution of requirements over the contract life

10. Jackson SPARKLE Model

The SPARKLE model identifies the core aspects required in the delivery of contract management, and added value. The model looks at the Stakeholders, the Contract Plan, the concept of "Adding value", the Risks involved, Key relationships in the team, development of a Long Term perspective and the compliance with Ethical best practice.

Developing a contractor relationship will usually follow a well-defined and documented path from identifying a need through to signature and into the performance phase of the contract. Measurement, evaluation and targets form an integral part in the process. However at certain moments in the contract development and execution cycle there are opportunities to turn a standard contract into a special relationship. These are the moments when the Contract Manager can make the contract "SPARKLE".

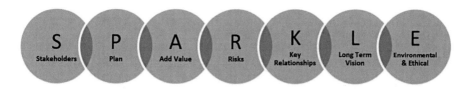

Stakeholders – Understand the needs of the main stakeholders.
Plan – Plan must address the core objectives and critical success factors.
Add Value – Focus on delivery and adding value.
Risk – Risk management and regular assessment is essential.
Key Relationships – Focus on the key relationships.
Long Term Vision – Develop vision, anticipation and forecasting.
Ethical and Environmental – Ensure ethical issues are considered.

Management of the contract is often an ongoing and testing role, however attention to these core elements will help ensure success.

Positive Views on Model	Negative Views on Model
• Highlights the core issues in Contract Management • Identifies and focuses on adding value	• No reference to contract development process • No review or feedback loop

11. KOTLER 8 PHASES OF CHANGE

The Kotler 8 Phases model considers change in 8 steps from the start through to making the change permanent.

The Kotler model breaks the process of change into 8 steps or phases from the initial preparation for work through to the difficult matter of making the change "stick".

The Kotler model begins by generating momentum with stakeholders, before building coalitions to ensure support from key areas. The project must have a clear vision around which stakeholders can unite with this vision and other key components effectively communicated. Once this is in place, delivery commences with a good project manager looking for quick wins to cement support and gather a momentum to the end of the project, with efforts at the conclusion to prevent reversion to the "old ways".

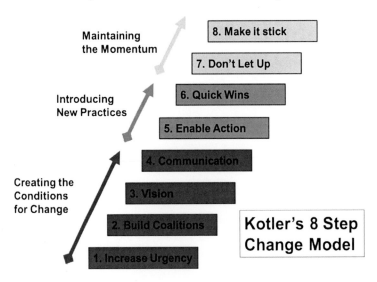

Positive Views on Model	Negative Views on Model
• Good systematic approach that increases success • Reduces the often inevitable resistance to change	• Needs management support and strong leadership • Being a systematic process, it's not very flexible

12. Lewin Freeze Model

The Lewin Freeze Model identifies the three core stages of successfully implementing and cementing change within an organisation. First it is necessary to unfreeze the status quo, before implementing the change, and refreezing the modified set–up or processes.

The Freeze Model is used to modify behaviours through unfreezing the activity or process, implementing the change and then refreezing to cement the change introduced.

Implementing change without the necessary preparation and "warming" of the team, merely leads to anguish and stress, the change fails to break the habit, and reversion to the old processes is then often inevitable. Organisations, and more importantly the individuals therein, need to be aware of the change, be enlightened as to the reasons and benefits of the change, and have a clearly identified pathway or project plan.

Once the organisation has been warmed – or unfrozen – to the idea of change, then the project activity can occur with the results more likely to be accepted. Once implemented, the amended system, process or structure needs to be refrozen, made the formal practice and embedded in the organisation's *modus operandi* with amendments made to the organisations operating procedures and process manual where necessary.

Note however, Nadler and Tushman suggested that different approaches for delivering change are required in different scenarios.

Positive Views on Model	Negative Views on Model
• Simple model with clear objectives and process • Shows the importance of embedding change	• Some would argue it is merely a common sense approach to warm the people who will be affected by the change.

SECTION 3 //ENVIRONMENTAL

- Carter STOPWASTE Model
- 8R Model of Responsible Waste Treatment
- Jackson Sustainability Impact Model
- Jackson Nine Dimensions of Sustainability
- Three E Model

13. Carter STOPWASTE Model

The Carter STOPWASTE Model looks at ways an organisation can reduce the waste it generates, be that physical waste, time, effort or some other facet.

S • Standardisation - Variety and choice leads to waste

T • Transport Mode - Is the transportation necessary or efficient?

O • Outsource - Is the activity the best use of OUR resources?

P • Process Reengineering - Could we improve the process?

W • Weight & Materials - Are weight and materials optimised?

A • Acquisition Costs - Are the procurement costs under control?

S • Specification - Is the specification correct and fit for purpose?

T • Take out Gold Plate - Are there avoidable "frills" in the design?

E • Elimination - Can anything be removed and not affect the value?

The STOPWASTE model is an acronym of nine ways an organisation can eliminate waste or cost from its operation. For example, reducing choice through the elimination of a standardised approach stops waste through:
- Lower levels of inventory;
- Improved compatibility and less time selecting products or services;
- Reduced downtime as a result of faster maintenance and repair;
- Lower levels of training and technical support.

Positive Views on Model	Negative Views on Model
• Alternative approach to identify waste in an organisation • Functional mnemonic	• No directive actions or process • Some waste reduction may have a knock-on impact

14. THE 8R MODEL OF RESPONSIBLE WASTE TREATMENT

The 8R Model is a sustainability model which highlights the eight main ways product or materials can be managed to extend life, or reduce waste; the most commonly cited "Rs" are Reduce, Reuse and Recycle.

The 8R Model highlights eight possible ways to manage waste product reaching the end of its operational life. The traditional model of Reduce, Reuse and Recycle has been adapted with an aim to help highlight alternative options for items to extend their useful life.

Whilst in many cases an item may be considered waste to one individual, it may still be serviceable to another. Selling or donating through concepts such as Ebay or Freecycle can locate a new user and extend the life of the product. Equally, remarketing with words such as retro, vintage or antique, or remanufacturing it to extend its life (e.g. remoulding tyres) is also useful.

8R's	Description	Example
Reuse	Reuse item in its intended role	Second hand items, e.g. clothes, cars, equipment
Resell	Resell item for use by another	Ebay and other classified ad sales channels
Removal	Remove from the market for storage	Old fire-engines are kept in storage for use in major incidents or during strike action.
Remarket	Remarket the item in a new light	At a certain age an old car becomes "vintage" and furniture becomes antique
Return to Manufacturer	Return item for raw material recovery	Stock cleanse items, old equipment, project surplus materials
Reclaim	Extraction of components for repairs or production	BAE Systems "Reduce to Produce" programme recovers serviceable parts out of old aircraft
Remanufacture	Re-manufacture to extend the life of the product	Re-treading of car tyres, refilling of gas cylinders
Recycle	Recover raw materials from an end of life asset	Scrap metal dealers, rare earth metal recovery from electronic items

Positive Views on Model	Negative Views on Model
• Useful *aide memoire* • Drives initiatives	• There are other solutions not included in the 8R list

15. Jackson Sustainability Impact Model

The Jackson Sustainability Impact Model looks at the areas where an organisation can positively and negatively impact on its sustainable dynamic. The acronym reflects: Inputs into the organisation; Minimisation of waste; People in the organisation; Asset utilisation; Use and management of Cash; and Time.

The Jackson Sustainability Impact Model looks at the sources of sustainable opportunity or squander within the organisation with these representing the areas which an organisation can look at to improve its sustainable credentials, with the acronym letters relating to the following:

I is for "Inputs" – Typically, procurement drives the acquisition of materials, services, finance and goodwill consumed by the organisation.

M is for "Minimise Waste" – This includes scrap, left-overs, off-cuts, quality failures as well as producing something the customer rejects.

P is for "People" – Without people, commitment and experience, an organisation will flounder. There must be an ambition to develop and retain the workforce and generate a steady stream of future talent.

A is for "Asset utilisation" – Whilst financial considerations are important for an organisation, what is often overlooked is the need to ensure that assets already owned by the organisation are used wherever possible.

C is for "Cash" – Essential to the ongoing success of an organisation is the need to create, or in a public authority effectively consume, cash.

T is for Time – And finally, the concept of time must not be overlooked as a key determinant of sustainability; it goes to the very core of the concept.

Positive Views on Model	Negative Views on Model
• Simple model • Analyses over time, not as a snapshot	• May not cover every facet to be considered • Does not drive clear direction

16. JACKSON NINE DIMENSIONS OF SUSTAINABILITY

The Nine Dimensions model expands the traditional Triple Bottom Line or Three Pillar model to add definition to each Pillar: the People Pillar considers Character, Company and Community (C); the Profit Pillar looks at Sales, Service and Strategy (S); and the Planet Pillar adopts Reduce, Reuse and Recycle (R).

The Triple Bottom Line model is an established model which suggests sustainability can be considered using three pillars labelled – Social, Economic and Environmental, or People, Profit and Planet, and subsequently has been expanded to help illustrate the core elements which make a strong pillar, and help students expand exam answers.

The People Pillar needs to consider the needs of the person or **Character**, its own **Company** requirements and the needs of the wider **Community** to ensure a long term supply of future employees and suppliers.

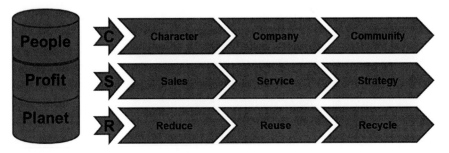

Equally there are three dimensions which are required to make a sustainable profit – a strong **Sales** structure, a good **Service** delivery to maintain the customers, and a **Strategy** to ensure that the profit is maintained over the period – and three considerations to ensure best use of natural resources – **Reducing** what is used, **Reusing** where possible and **Recycling** product and/or raw materials.

Positive Views on Model	Negative Views on Model
• Highlights how the *Pillars* and thus a CSR policy can be developed and made effective	• No indication of what should be in each dimension or how the CSR process and policy should be constructed

17. Three E Model

The Three E Model is used to pinpoint and evaluate cost reduction opportunities. These prospective cost reduction ideas will fall generally into one of three areas – Economic, Efficiency, and Effectiveness.

The three different ways of reducing cost in a project generally fall into one of three categories:

- Economic – Obtain a lower cost for the product or service;
- Efficiency – Get more return from the product or service;
- Effectiveness – Use the product or service in a more strategic way.

Economy	Efficiency	Effectiveness
• The cost of procuring and using the goods or services • In the lighting example, the cost of the electrical power to run the lighting system	• The comparison between what is and what could have been • In the lighting example, choice of light sources will affect the quantity of the light emitted per KWh of power	• The extent to which the objectives are achieved • In the lighting example, this might include the strategic timing or placement of light fittings

This is perhaps best explained with an example:

In order to reduce the costs of lighting in a building we could:

1. Lower the price of a unit of electricity (Economy)
2. Make the light sources emit more light for the same power (Efficiency)
3. Use the lighting only when required or in core locations (Effectiveness)

Positive Views on Model	Negative Views on Model
• Easy and simple to remember model useful to identify issues opportunities	• Doesn't focus on structural cost reduction, CAPEX reduction or consequential costs

Section 4 // General Management

- Ansoff Planning Model
- Ashridge Management Styles
- Balanced Scorecards
- Critical Needs Analysis (CNA)
- Fayol Principles of Management
- Greiner Growth Model
- Hersey–Blanchard Model
- Hierarchy of Objectives
- Jackson Fraud and Corruption Plan
- Johnson Supplier Management Behaviour Model
- McKinsey7S Model
- Mintzberg 5P Model
- Pareto Analysis
- PEST / PESTLE / STEEPLE / STEEPLED Analysis
- RACI Assessment
- Rogers Seven Point Plan
- Senge Five Disciplines
- SMART Objectives
- SWOT Analysis & TOWS Strategy Model

18. Ansoff Planning Model

The Ansoff Planning Model is used to identify planning requirements and process within an organisation as well as establishing review and monitoring process to enable improved control of the business activities – remember If you can't measure it, you can't manage it!

The Ansoff Planning Model steps through the managerial planning process, through the initial stages of analysis, to identifying opportunity, selection of options, final decision-making and implementation.

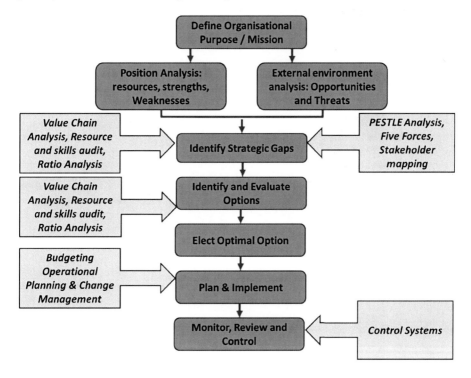

The model incorporates the critical review and feedback loops and can also use the other major models to generate inputs throughout as shown.

Positive Views on Model	Negative Views on Model
• Draws models into the planning process • Generates a clear end product	• Often difficult for practitioners to associate with

19. ASHRIDGE MANAGEMENT STYLES

The Ashridge Management Styles focus on how a leader delivers a message to a team and identifies four classic types of message conveyance: Tells, Sells, Consults and Joins.

The Ashridge model identifies four core styles of transmitting message from management to the employees. Each style has its time and place and certain organisations, industries or operations may have a tendency towards one particular style.

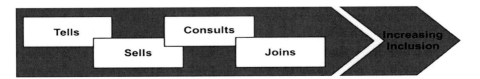

Tells – The leader tells the team players what needs to occur. There is no dialogue, orders are given – imagine a General in the army, for example, he or she will most likely adopt a "Tell" solution due to the strict hierarchical structure.

Sells – The leader uses selling skills to highlight the benefits of following the commands. They would have an answer for any objections and negate *objectors*, they would carefully use open and closed questions and would focus on obtaining a decision.

Consults – The leader would use consultation to obtain ideas and some buy-in. The ideas would then be fashioned into a proposal and then delivered. There would be buy-in as a result of the process as people know that the outcome reflects the team's ideas.

Joins – A far more collaborative process where identified team players discuss options, arrange process, agree direction and implement as a unified body; some Scandinavian organisations adopt a high level of "Joins" to ensure total buy-in to a project solution.

Positive Views on Model	Negative Views on Model
• Highlights four distinct methods of communication and identifies the impact and consequences of each	• Assumes that management–subordinate relationships act the same in every scenario • No reflection of criticality or risk

20. BALANCED SCORECARDS

The Kaplan and Norton (1992) Balanced Scorecard is a robust and structured report underpinned with well-established processes and methods. It is used by organisations to measure, manage and verify performance across a number of core business facets.

The Balanced Scorecard was conceived by Robert Kaplan and David Norton with a focus on developing performance measures that are based on aspects other than just financial return. These additional measures include analysis of the success of customer interaction, the effectiveness and suitability of internal business processes, and how it treats and utilises its employees and highlight what should be measured and managed, with assessments of targets and objectives.

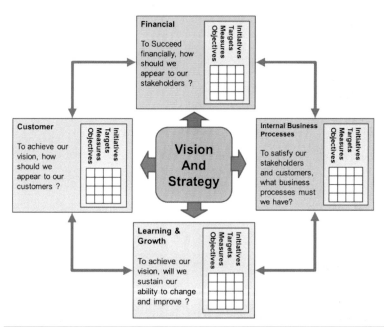

Positive Views on Model	Negative Views on Model
• Gives an overall view of the health of the organisation • Flexible to suit the specific needs of the business	• May distract from the financial requirements • Can be hard to create metrics if they are subjective

21. CRITICAL NEEDS ANALYSIS (CNA)

Critical Needs Analysis is used to determine the critical features necessary for the supply or production of an item or service to ensure it has all necessary features yet is not over-engineered or gold-plated. The item or service shall endeavour to be just "Fit for Purpose".

In a Critical Needs Analysis evaluation, all the needs are listed and categorised as either primary functions or secondary functions, no other features will then affect the determination of the chosen solution. The approach needs a cross-functional methodology to avoid a skewed perspective and should maintain a non–supplier specific perspective. This process should be used as a forerunner to the production of a specification so demands a diverse stakeholder input and should not – especially in a public sector environment – involve any supplier involvement. For example consider the selection of a writing implement.

Score 1-5 weighed x2 for primary factors and x1 for secondary factors.	Primary	Needs		Secondary Needs				
	Cost	Cost of Ink	Quality of ink	Flexibility	Leakage	Versatility	Ergonomics	Transportable	Totals
Ball Point Pen	4	4	2	4	4	5	3	4	44
Fountain Pen	1	3	5	4	2	3	4	3	38
Roller Ball Pen	3	4	4	5	4	3	3	3	45
Fibre Tip	4	2	2	3	5	3	2	4	36
Pencil	5	5	1	3	5	3	3	5	44
Feather Quill	1	3	3	1	5	1	1	2	25

Positive Views on Model	Negative Views on Model
• Drives the inclusion of only "Value Added" aspects of a design • Allows the Weighting of options • Enables prioritisation of needs	• Needs diverse input to be effective • Ignores other needs that may evolve • May not appreciate all the options leading to possible idea stagnation

22. FAYOL PRINCIPLES OF MANAGEMENT

The Fayol Principles of Management identifies the 14 characteristics that are key traits of a successful manager and aspects that they must address.

Fayol identified 14 aspects that are critical for a successful manager to focus on and address, i.e. the things a manager should ensure happen as a norm within their organisational remit.

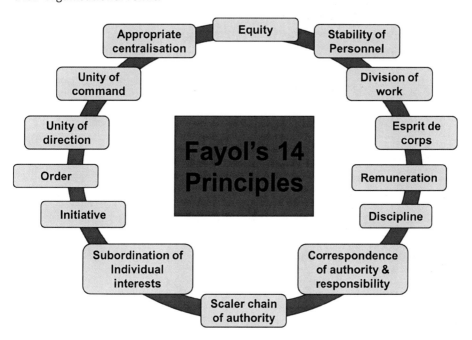

Clearly aspects such as "discipline", "recognition of the managerial authority" and "personnel issues" are core but "showing initiative" and "generating a clear direction" are activities where the manager has a leadership responsibility and are of equal importance.

Positive Views on Model	Negative Views on Model
• Identifies the core elements of a day to day management role • Good for mechanistic activities with a clear hierarchy of control	• Fails to address strategic activities or vision • Very 'now' focused; low future–proofing

23. GREINER GROWTH MODEL

The Greiner Growth Model identifies six distinct stages within an organisation's expansion and recognises this growth cycle will encounter clear evidence of "crisis" caused by the catalyst driving the evolution.

The Greiner Growth Model identified six areas of growth starting with the early creativity or development of the new idea or business concept. This flows through until there is a leadership crisis when the size of the business demands a review of the management structure.

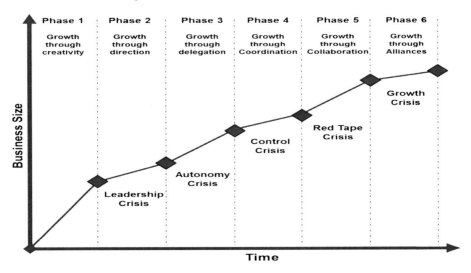

Once appointed, the management team will enable the organisation to grow under their guidance, yet there comes a time when the workers need autonomy to guide themselves; this is the autonomy crisis. Next comes a phase where delegation is adopted to allow workers to be self–directed but this leads to a control crisis due to a lack of centralised control that is remedied by a phase of coordination which prevails until red tape stifles the business. Finally, the red tape is overcome through a period of collaboration which generates issues over the internal growth of the organisation leading to strategic alliances.

Positive Views on Model	Negative Views on Model
• Highlights the problems that occur with business growth • Helps dismantle issues	• Not all organisations grow in the same way or timescales • Doesn't reflect market issues

24. HERSEY BLANCHARD MODEL

Hersey Blanchard suggested that "Change Leadership" depends upon (1) the maturity of the participants, (2) the maturity of the staff for the task and (3) upon how ready the Stakeholders are to adopt change.

Hersey Blanchard considered the type of people in a team or organisation, and tried to assess how ready for leadership roles they were. He concluded that the maturity of the people will determine the way that change is delivered or managed. This may result in the type of team leader selected, whether the leader comes from within the organisation or is recruited without any pre–conceived ideas, without any legacy or baggage, or whether the participants respect prior knowledge or history within the incumbent organisation.

The model suggests the manner in which the team participants are managed, communicated with and led is important. Hersey Blanchard suggested that in some circumstance – for example military commanders – management will be through "telling" the team players what to do, with little or no room for subordinate input. Equally, there were some circumstances where the participants should be more closely involved – as is typical in co-operatives or many Japanese organisations.

Telling	**M1**
Selling	**M2**
Participating	**M3**
Delegating	**M4**

The levels of maturity are labelled M1-M4 with the higher number being those who are more operationally mature, more willing to change.

Positive Views on Model	Negative Views on Model
• Helps management identify the best way to communicate with its workforce • Identifies when engagement with staff will work best	• Doesn't reflect specific nature of the issue in question • Ignores the untapped resource of the employees • Doesn't differentiate between leadership and management

25. HIERARCHY OF OBJECTIVES

Procurement competence is the *"capability to structure the supply base in alignment with the business priorities of the organisation"*. An effective procurement function needs therefore to coordinate and align procurement plans, policies and actions to the overall strategic business objectives.

The author Philip Boulton proposes that procurement's contribution to business performance depends on the degree to which procurement capabilities fit and support the business strategy. This highlights the importance of procurement strategy as an intermediate element between business strategy and procurement capabilities.

Mission Statement	Purpose, business area, key values
Organisational Goals	Desired future state, where we want to be
Specific Objectives	Specific targets, what we need to do
Strategic Plans	Broad direction, long term 3-5years
Tactical Plans	Medium term plans, 1-2 years
Operational Plans	Departmental plans, short term 1 year

Positive Views on Model	Negative Views on Model
• Gives clear structure to goal and objective setting • Ensures all goals are aligned across the organisation	• Reduces the focus on individual requirements and making targets SMART • Puts organisation needs ahead of the employee need

26. JACKSON FRAUD AND CORRUPTION PLAN

The Fraud and Corruption Plan highlights the need for organisations to manage risks associated with Fraud and Corruption in their operation. This continuum requires constant review, management, reporting and training to ensure employees understand the importance of the issue.

The enactment of a Fraud and Corruption Plan starts with a definition of what constitutes fraud and corruption, which may differ between cultures and operating spheres. Once defined, the organisation needs to review its current status to identify the risks it faces and create a Fraud and Corruption Plan.

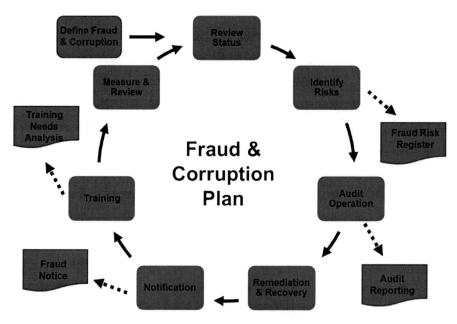

Once there is a plan and the personnel have been informed, audits, remediation and recovery activities can be put in place with notifications and training where necessary. Once informed and trained there is no longer any reason why an employee should breach the guidelines, however with any such activity, there needs to be a constant review and feedback loop to ensure continued adherence and compliance.

Positive Views on Model	Negative Views on Model
• Clearly defined anti–corruption process with audit and reporting	• Can have other steps such as "naming and shaming"

27. JOHNSON SUPPLIER MANAGEMENT BEHAVIOUR MODEL

The Johnson Supplier Management Behaviour Model looks at how effective SRM can deliver benefit through a solid supplier management approach that reflects the difficulty of the market and duration of the contract to lock in value from sourcing often lost in post-contract activity.

The Johnson Supplier Management Behaviour Model looks at client organisational behaviour towards suppliers by matching *Market Difficulty* with *Anticipated duration of relationship or probability of re–engagement.*

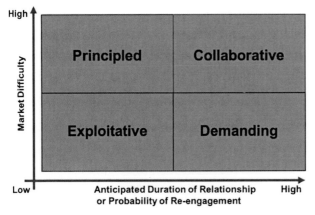

Principled There is little possibility of long term relationships forming and few potential suppliers. A mixture of persuasion and firm negotiation is needed to develop preferred suppliers in order to leverage opportunities.

Collaboration High chance of long-term relationships whereby both parties spend time to build trust and develop mutually beneficial interfaces.

Exploitation Limited long term relationships, so gain maximum benefits from leverage using competition and playing the spot market.

Demanding High possibility of long term relationships with preferred supplier status. Competition used for benchmarking purposes with buyers looking to develop closer relationships. The model is useful for categorising client behaviours, but is limited by the consideration of only two variables.

Positive Views on Model	Negative Views on Model
• Focuses on relationship behaviour to add optimum value	• Only considers two variables

28. McKinsey 7S Model

The McKinsey 7S model focuses on a network of seven inter-related core elements that if combined effectively ensures that optimal performance occurs. These elements are divided into tangible, easy to define elements (hard) and others which are less definable (soft) elements.

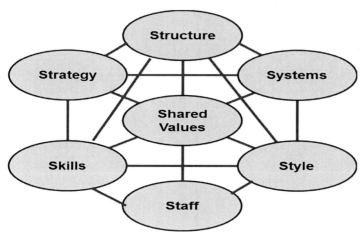

- **Structure** – An organisation with a clear and considered **Structure** will perform better, be more flexible and will reduce risk;
- **Systems** – Like structure, organised, tried and tested **Systems** will help improve performance, however compliance is also vital;
- **Style** – The **Style** of leadership can be important and needs to reflect the nature of the organisation and its stakeholders;
- **Staff** – The quality, motivation and commitment of the **Staff** and employees or will have a major impact on the organisation's performance;
- **Skills** – Further, the staff need to be well trained and possess the necessary **Skills** to fulfil their job roles, and unanticipated risks;
- **Strategy** – An organisation will perform better and react to change more quickly if it has a coherent **Strategy** in place;
- **Shared Values** – And finally, ensuring that the values that exist within the organisation are **Shared** by the stakeholders.

Positive Views on Model	Negative Views on Model
• A good analysis framework • Tried, tested and extensively used model to develop strategy	• No clear outcomes just direction

29. Mintzberg 5P Model

The Mintzberg 5P Model identifies five core areas which need to be considered when developing a business strategy: Planning, Ploys, Patterns, Positioning and Perspective.

Minzberg suggested that there are five core areas around which a strategy is centred. Each is critical to delivery of a specific facet of the strategy and a failure to consider each will undermine its effectiveness:

1. **PLAN** – An organisation should be aware that strategic PLANning is one core requirement of an effective strategy. This should be a conscious, democratic and structured process;

2. **PLOY** – We can enhance a strategy by developing PLOYs to out manoeuvre our competitors, in much the same way a General might develop military tactics to outwit an enemy;

3. **PATTERN** – Further, a strategy could be generated based on our previous PATTERNs of behaviour, i.e. a strategy based on our experience of past activities or performance. A PATTERN may also involve collaboration between several activities to achieve the goal;

4. **POSITION** – Equally, we need to ensure that we adopt a clear and decisive POSITION in respect of our strategy or a specific point therein;

5. **PERSPECTIVE** – Finally, we need to understand how the views of others are affected by our strategy by considering their PERSPECTIVE or vision of the future events in the market or organisational life–cycle.

Positive Views on Model	Negative Views on Model
• Helps drive the thought process around the critical aspects which make a strategy successful	• Doesn't necessarily include all factors that are important: e.g. political pressure or previous experience • Doesn't include a review or feedback cycle

30. PARETO ANALYSIS

Pareto Analysis, often known as the 80:20 rule, suggests that 80% of the outcome will come from 20% of the causes. This can be shown using empirical analysis and is a phenomenon commonly seen in nature.

The Pareto or 80:20 rule is a commonly referred to concept in business, mathematics, economics, as well as many sciences and in nature. It suggests that 80% of an output will come from 20% of the inputs, for example, 80% of sales will come from 20% of the customers, 80% of the deliveries will come from 20% of the inventory, 80% of accidents will be attributed to just 20% of the risks, etc.

The Pareto Principle can be explained mathematically (Reference Power Law Distribution Concept model outside the scope of this book), but was originally identified through observation of natural occurrences such as 80% of land in Italy was owned by 20% of the population, 80% of a crop will come from 20% of the seed, 80% of wealth comes from 20% of the population, etc.

In business, the Pareto concept is seen regularly where statistical analysis is used, for example, inventory management activities, Six Sigma, in Activity Based Costing models, forecasting and projection models, etc.

In inventory, it is used alongside other concepts – for example the Normal Distribution – to help eliminate dead or excess stock, to improve service levels, plan warehouse locations, assign inventory categories, etc. In a customer-facing warehouse for example, fast moving A stock (the top 20% of products which will account for 80% of the sales and thus 80% of the stock picks) should be located nearest to the sales counter to help reduce customer waiting time, and sales staff distance travelled to pick an item.

Positive Views on Model	Negative Views on Model
• Well-established natural occurrence • Used in many statistical applications across the business	• Doesn't work well with low numbers of inputs or outputs • Rarely exactly 80% so needs to still be calculated • Other models exist such as Theil index

31. PEST / PESTLE / STEEPLE / STEEPLED Analysis

The PEST, PESTLE, STEEPLE and STEEPLED acronym models are used to assess the external environment in which the organisation operates. PEST (Political, Economic, Social, Technical) was the original model but grew to form PESTLE (with Legislation and Environmental) which has, itself, grown in recent times to indicate Ethical factors giving an extra E and a D for Demographics making the word STEEPLED.

The STEEPLED model looks at the external aspects that can affect an organisation. These include:

- **S – Social Factors** – People and community issues such as the standard of living, welfare, happiness;
- **T – Technical Factors** – The level of technology in the market, technical complexity of product or components, software issues etc;
- **E – Economic Factors** – These may include the value of currency, GDP rates, minimum wage, debt levels, unemployment, etc;
- **E – Environmental Factors** – These may recognise issues with climate change or global warming, use of resources, pollution, etc;
- **P – Political Factors** – May include aspects such as a change in government or political ethos, electorate swings, or dominant leaders;
- **L – Legislation** – Will address changes in laws, trade restrictions, the position taken by the judiciary, etc;
- **E – Ethical Issues** – including corruption, extortion, bribery, collusion, dubious sources of finance, reducing child labour, etc.
- **D – Demographical Issues** – including population size, makeup, education, and behaviours of the population.

This model encourages thorough consideration of external aspects that could affect the organisation both positively and negatively.

Positive Views on Model	Negative Views on Model
• Simple but internationally recognised acronym checklist • Useful checklist for someone considering external factors	• Model has evolved but many still use PEST/PESTLE and do not recognise SLEPT, STEEPLE or STEEPLED

32. RACI Assessment

The RACI (Responsible, Accountable, Consulted and Informed) philosophy focuses on clarifying what stakeholders' roles are and their responsibilities in the context of the specific task or process step.

The main application of the RACI matrix may be used to:
- Specify the involvement of various stakeholders in a project;
- Supplement the Stakeholder power/interest analysis.

The approach works best when the following are adopted:

- There is only one **Accountable** person to avoid confusion;
- Limited **Responsible** persons involved to one to avoid duplication;
- A **Responsible** and an **Accountable** person must be assigned to every level of activity;
- Confirms the roles and activities assigned with all stakeholders.

Positive Views on Model	Negative Views on Model
• Gives stakeholders clarity about roles and responsibilities • Ensures each activity has all the RACI roles assigned	• Does not assign relationships between stakeholders • Responsibility often over used only apply to a single person

33. ROGERS SEVEN POINT PLAN

The Rogers Seven Point Plan identifies seven core areas that need to be explored in the recruitment process, such as intelligence, background, skills, attainment, attitude, physical ability and life interests.

The Rogers Seven Point Plan recognises the core elements that need to be assessed in a recruitment process, to ensure that the individual selected meets the needs of the business at an operational, intellectual, physical and motivational level. The model considers the following seven points that need consideration:

- **Intelligence** – The intelligence of the person
- **Background** – The person's background
- **Attainment** – Their attainment
- **Aptitude** – Special aptitudes or skills
- **Interests** – The candidate's personal interests
- **Physical** – The person's physical condition
- **Disposition** – The person's disposition

Ideally all of these areas should be explored through effective questioning or assessments in the interview process to establish whether the person is fit for purpose both in the short, medium and over the longer term.

Furthermore, the job role or specification is an integral part of the process and will need to be considered in how this is achieved as some roles will be more likely to evolve over time. In such circumstances higher levels of intelligence and the right disposition would be required and the individual may require a background that is more accommodating to development, learning and change.

Positive Views on Model	Negative Views on Model
• Provides a clear statement of core areas that need assessing in the interview process. • Gives guidance when determining interview strategy	• No tie-in to other models such as Belbin or other team accredited models.

34. SENGE FIVE DISCIPLINES

The Senge Five Disciplines theory identifies the five core leadership disciplines which are considered useful when implementing change recognising that during such times there is a need to harness all the skills of the workforce and enable them to learn and develop.

The Senge Five Disciplines theory considers the critical need for an organisation to cultivate the learning potential of its workforce during a time of change and maintain their commitment during a time of potentially heightened stress. Recognising this, Senge proposed the five primary leadership skills necessary to harness this learning and commitment:

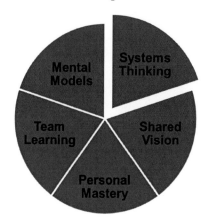

- **Shared Vision** – Helps build commitment and reduces resistance
- **Personal Mastery** – Helps people become self-aware and builds confidence in their own ability
- **Team Learning** – Helps group learning by confronting change in unity
- **Mental Models** – Develops beliefs, values, anxieties and perceptions over the change process
- **Systems Vision** – Increases awareness of the change programme and how it impacts on the organisation, and it unites all the disciplines

Positive Views on Model	Negative Views on Model
• Identifies the leadership focus to effect successful change • Disciplines united by Systems Vision so effort often in tandem	• Learning cultures and environments take time to develop

35. SMART Objectives

The SMART model looks at the characteristics of an effective operational target. The target should be Specific, Measurable, Achievable, Relevant and Timed. Using SMART targets increases engagement and the successful attainment of the desired outcome.

SMART targets are considered more effective and conducive to achievement and improving performance. These features should therefore be considered whenever setting corporate or personal goals and targets.

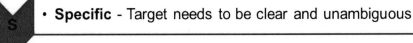

S • **Specific** - Target needs to be clear and unambiguous

M • **Measurable** - Target needs to have a clear measure and an undisputed data source

A • **Achievable** - The target must be achievable as otherwise it will demotivate

R • **Relevant** - The target must be relevant to the organisation and add some obvious value to its goals

T • **Timed** - Target must have a starting point, and a finishing point

Whilst this model is generally recognised as being thus, in some circumstances the letters have been adjusted – for example Realistic sometimes replaces Relevant or Attainment instead of Achievable – yet the method and concept remains the same, to effectively set the goals and achieve them.

Positive Views on Model	Negative Views on Model
• Simple, recognised, effective and understood • Commonplace and regularly used model	• Letters sometimes changed • Other options – such as the six–point plan – used in some circumstances

36. SWOT Analysis & TOWS Strategy Model

A SWOT Analysis is used to assess the internal capabilities of an organisation to understand its ability to perform in a particular scenario. The TOWS model was a later extension to the SWOT model which sought to generate or drive the formulation of a strategy from the SWOT findings.

The SWOT Analysis was developed by the Stanford Research Institute and is used to analyse the capabilities of an organisation to compete and capitalise on corporate opportunities. It is used to identify an organisation's strengths, weaknesses, opportunities and threats:

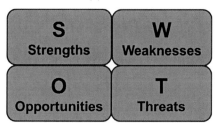

The TOWS model goes further turning the SWOT Analysis into a functional strategy development tool that reflects issues and actions required associated with each intersect:

	Opportunities External Positive Impacts	Threats External Negative Impacts
Strengths Internal Positive Impacts	Utilise the strengths in the most effective way to capitalise upon the opportunities	Utilise the strengths of the organisation to combat against and minimise the impact of the threats
Weaknesses Internal Negative Impacts	Address the weaknesses in the organisation that prevent it from capitalising on the opportunities	Create strategy to minimise the organisation's weaknesses to protect it against the threats

Positive Views on Model	Negative Views on Model
• SWOT model widely recognised and commonly used model • Easy to understand and implement	• SWOT does not deliver a clear strategy • TOWS relatively unknown and used less that SWOT

Section 5 // Human Resource Management

- Adair Action–Centred Leadership Model
- Adizes Management Profiles
- Belbin Team Roles
- Crocker Triangle
- Handy Organisational Culture Model
- Herzberg Hygiene/Motivators
- Hofstede Cultural Factors Model
- Jackson POINT Model
- Jackson RITUAL
- Johnson Cultural Web
- Lewin Force Field Analysis
- Maslow Hierarchy of Needs
- Mintzberg Management Roles
- Theory X, Theory Y and Theory Z
- Tuckman Team Development Cycle

37. ADAIR ACTION CENTRED LEADERSHIP MODEL

Adair identified three specific characteristics that are important when looking at the management of an organisation: The Task, The Group dynamics and the Individuals therein. The model suggests that leadership can be learned, and people are not necessarily born leaders.

Adair's research was based at Sandhurst Military Training Academy in 1979 and focused on the leadership of a group concluded that there are three specific facets which hold importance – Task, Group and Individuals – and that leadership **can** be taught and is **not** determined at birth.

The overlap areas between the three characteristics are important areas of development and where management focus can effect change and create dynamic value.

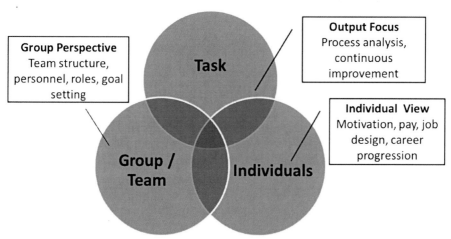

For example, team bonding is clearly a major part of the Group or Team element, however improving this will help enhance the contribution and commitment of the individual. Equally, the delivery of output on time, quality and budget will be greatly enhanced if there is a team commitment.

Positive Views on Model	Negative Views on Model
• Highlights the core elements of a great leader • Helps focus on core aspects	• Works best in an autocratic environment • Some view this as outdated and over simplistic

38. Adizes Management Profiles

The Adizes Management Profiles concept suggests that the act of management has four core dimensions — Producer, Administrator, Entrepreneur and Integrator — with fractures occurring if the manager has a deficiency in any one facet referred to as the "Mis-Management Crisis".

Adizes suggested that an optimal manager needs to be somewhat proficient in all four of the management areas otherwise they will show features of what he called "mis–management".

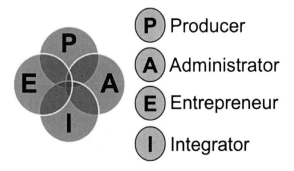

P	Producer
A	Administrator
E	Entrepreneur
I	Integrator

Adizes believes that every manager has a primary style or styles which are denoted by a capital letter, if they recognise and accept other managerial traits this will be reflected with a lower case. For example a manager may have risen through the ranks, worked hard and become good at ensuring activities occur on time and quality; making him a Producer. He may also recognise the need for integrating change, understand that the admin function is necessary and know he needs people in the team who seize opportunities — he would therefore have a managerial style of Pael.

Any manager who fails to recognise the need of a particular managerial style would receive a dash — for example P–el. This dash identifies a risk as he or she may mismanage any activities in this dimension of the business, whilst a manager proficient in all aspects would be a PAEI.

Positive Views on Model	Negative Views on Model
• Long recognised model • Simple and easily identified behaviours	• Sits in an area with a lot of different views • Weak areas can be hidden through strong recruitment

39. Belbin Team Roles

Belbin identified and examined the different roles that people take within an team or organisation. Belbin categorised these into Action, Social and Thinking roles with individuals having a tendency to trend towards one main role.

Belbin recognised that when formulating a team it is critical to ensure that there is a blend of roles within the team, and that each individual had a tendency towards a certain role behaviour. Having all of one type of role type in a team will lead to an unbalanced team and often result in skewed results and outcomes, such instances in history include the "Bay of Pigs" incident in Cuba and arguably the "Second Iraq War".

Action	Social	Thinking

Action
- Completer Finisher - Focuses on what is required to complete the project
- Implementer - Drives the implementation of ideas within the team
- Shaper - Steers direction and scope of the project or team activity

Social
- Co-ordinator – Co-ordinates people and resources within the team
- Resource Instigator - Ensures all resources are obtained as required
- Team Worker - Supports team activity, willing to undertake tasks

Thinking
- Monitor Evaluator - Manages milestones, objectives and measurement
- Specialist - Team player who has specialist skills or technical input
- Plant – Generates ideas and direction of the project

In a project setting, if the team is full of specialists, for example, there is a chance that the project will not be finished or will be delivered late. If a team is full of monitor evaluators, then the team will be worried about progress and quality and less focused on idea generation or deadlines.

Positive Views on Model	Negative Views on Model
• Identifies core instinct of people • Improves balance of teams	• Rarely used as a starting point when developing teams • Individual may mask core nature for personal reasons

40. CROCKER TRIANGLE

The Crocker Triangle examines the enormous savings and operational opportiunities that can be made by Procurement facilitating the use of internal and external Cross-functional Teams (CFTs).

The Crocker Triangle highlights the inter-relationships between client internal operations, the client's user interface and the service provider and highlights the activity required to add value in each of the three direct interactions shown on the three arrows.

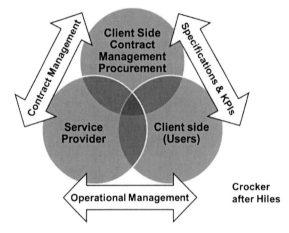

Crocker
after Hiles

Internally, close co-operation between Procurement, Production, Finance and R&D, alongside external interactions with Suppliers, can result in benefits in three key areas:

- **Leverage buying power** (Renegotiating contracts and re-bundling volumes)
- **Leverage product improvements** (standardisation, design to cost and value analysis)
- **Optimise processes** (reduce joint costs and waste reduction)

Positive Views on Model	Negative Views on Model
• Aligns internal relationships with team activity • Highlights operational activity needed to add the value	• Other areas such as risk need to be addressed using other models in parallel

41. HANDY ORGANISATIONAL CULTURE MODEL

The Handy Organisational Culture Model breaks down an organisation's culture into four distinct areas: Power Culture, Task Culture, Role Culture and the Support (or HR/People) Culture. The model shows how each element is embedded into the structure of the wider organisation's culture.

The Handy Organisational Culture Model identifies four main types of organisational culture reflecting both (1) the dynamic nature of the organisation, the market or the operating climate and (2) the complexity of the business activity, production process or product. These cultures were referred to as: Power, Role, Task and Person although Handy also assigned Roman gods to each for ease of recognition and learning.

	Power(Zeus) Culture reflects the main players in the organisation, i.e. those with the power, this culture is usually dynamic, controlled from the centre but it can be quite simplistic	Task(Athen) Culture relates to products or services being produced and how this is achieved. Can often be very dynamic and complex to reflect changes in the product being produced
Rate of Change	Role (Apollo) Culture and structure often quite stable, bureaucratic and with low levels of change. Will often involve defined processes and job functions especially if the task is predictable	Person(Dionysius) Culture tends to focus on individuals rather than the whole and is often seen where the organisation is dependent on specialist expertise who believe they are indispensable

Complexity of Work Activity

Each of the roles display different approaches to aspects such as change, written down and fixed processes, quality and teamwork. For example, people who are at the centre of the Person quadrant tend to see aspects such as administrative activities as being beneath them, and so on.

Positive Views on Model	Negative Views on Model
• Links can be seen with leadership style • Structure often reflects culture	• Culture difficult to define • More than one type of culture may exist in an organisation

42. HERZBERG HYGIENE/MOTIVATORS

Herzberg identified two characteristics that apply to an individual, Hygiene factors (things expected to be present but dissatisfy if they are absent) and Motivators (things not expected but generate delight if they occur).

Herzberg recognised two core types of influence in a scenario which he called Hygiene and Motivators – Hygiene are the factors that you expect to be present. They will not delight you, but they will generate dissatisfaction if they are not there. In contrast there are Motivators – these are items that you do not expect, but which will delight you if they occur and will help generate positive feelings within the team.

Hygiene Factors	**Creates:**	In a bank you would expect there to be money available (Hygiene Factor) and would be dis-satisfied if there was not.
• **Management** • **Salary** • **Security** • **HES** • **Work Conditions**	• **Satisfaction** • **Reduced Dis-satisfaction**	

Motivator Factors	**Creates:**	Yet it would be a nice surprise if you were offered a cup of coffee whilst queuing (Motivator), but you would not be disappointed if you did not get one
• **Recognition** • **Interesting Role** • **Opportunities** • **Responsibility** • **Pride**	• **Motivation** • **Increased commitment** • **Greater satisfaction**	

Positive Views on Model	Negative Views on Model
• Long established and recognised model • Clearly identifies aspects which are considered as mandatory and marginal	• Hygiene and motivators could be user specific • Motivators can become hygiene factors over time • Marginal benefit can reduce over time

43. HOFSTEDE CULTURAL FACTORS MODEL

Hofstede identified five core characteristics of national identity: Power Distance; Long Term Perspective; Uncertainty Avoidance; Masculinity; and Individualism. Each nation he examined displayed tendencies towards different combinations of these traits and exhibited different weightings.

Understanding the typical people traits of a nation helps explain: the reaction to a suggestion such as a commercial pitch; the response you may receive from a new idea; the urgency with which a decision is made; the different reactions to male and female pressures; the power hierarchy; decision processes; time to get agreements; and so on. These can be seen at the website www.hofstede. com. For example:

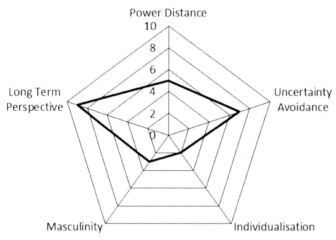

Take different nations with which you are familiar and compare them to the Hofstede model. Be careful with larger nations where there may be diverse characteristics, for example in Nigeria there are large tribal trends that differ from North to South which may skew any findings, or the United States where different states may have differing behaviours, for example compare Alaska with Arizona, Wyoming and West Virginia.

Positive Views on Model	Negative Views on Model
• Identifies characteristics with which many people can associate • Simple to identify general traits of a nation and avoid issues	• The model aggregates personality characteristics. • Model only looks at extreme characteristics

44. Jackson POINT Model

The Jackson POINT Model looks at the most effective way in which a piece of written information can be communicated. It considers the best way to make a message heard and for the audience to remember what was said. It considers *Preparation*, suggests a *One* page target, ensures the content is of *Interest* and *Newsworthy*, and complies with the concept of *Three*.

The Jackson POINT Model identifies that the critical aim when communicating – especially in the written form – is that the message is heard, understood and remembered. Failure on any of these three critical elements and the effort is worthless and the impacts are diminished.

The POINT model requires the following:

- **P – PREPARATION** – Good preparation and a deliver strategy such as the Point–Reason–Example–Point method used by politicians;
- **O – ONE PAGE** – Make any document one page, anymore and the message will be lost in the volume – a one page document will always be read before a book, and the secret to being remembered is to be first, second or last, one page helps ensure this;
- **I – INTERESTING** – Seems obvious, but make the text interesting otherwise it will go in one ear and out of the other;
- **N – NEWSWORTHY** – Try and tie the message into a recent event, a piece of news or the current corporate endeavour to add impact;
- **T – THREE** – Finally do not make it too complicated, use The Power of Three – A brain becomes muddled when there are more than three points, three colours (including the background even if it's white), sizes or types of test, etc., so help your readers brain function. And don't "right justify" text, this slows the reading down and reduce retention due to the variability of spacing between the letters exceeding, you've guessed it, three.

Positive Views on Model	Negative Views on Model
• Simple and effective • Structured *aide memoire*	• Communication is a skill • One page not always enough • Interesting is a user function

45. JACKSON RITUAL

Jackson RITUAL is an acronym model which looks at the HR cycle from recruitment to leaving. It helps highlight the importance of each element through the lifecycle of an employee – from Recruitment through Induction, Training, Utilisation, Appraisal and concluding with the Leaving – and drive initiatives to develop better induction or appraisal processes.

Jackson RITUAL assesses each phase of the employment cycle to highlight the importance of each component to the successful maintenance of an engaged and effective workforce.

The cycle commences with the recruitment of the employee, with attention to the job advertisement, the publication media, pre–interview correspondence, etc. This is followed with the Interview process which needs to assess the individual against structured criteria, (See model 33 Rogers 7 Point Plan). The employee is then trained, utilised and appraised (hopefully at least annually) throughout his career before final departure.

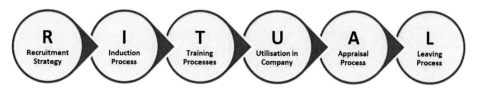

R	I	T	U	A	L
Recruitment Strategy	Induction Process	Training Processes	Utilisation in Company	Appraisal Process	Leaving Process

Following the cessation of activities, a leaver interview should be undertaken as valuable information can be obtained from leavers which may include dissatisfaction, salary or pay trends in the market, internal issues such as bullying or substandard personnel management, etc.

Positive Views on Model	Negative Views on Model
• Gives a clear end to end HR process to ensure best practice • Helps reduce staff turnover and improve morale	• Needs independent process for each element • No feedback loops included

46. Johnson Cultural Web

The Johnson "Cultural Web" (1987) identifies the aspects that drive the formation of the culture in an organisation, these include: Stories/Myths, Symbols, Power and Organisational Structure, Systems and Rituals.

The Cultural Web incorporates six aspects referred to as "Cultural Paradigms", these are considered aspects that generate culture in an organisation.

Understanding how the culture develops helps management steer or blend the culture by proactively or reactively changing the structures and processes in the organisation. This can be through changes to training, work-groups, recruitment, marketing, operating structure, processes, etc.

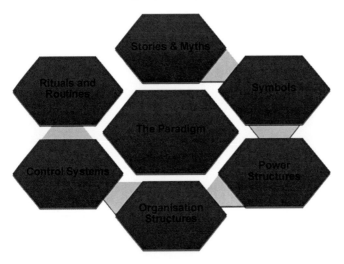

More difficult to address is the eradication of negative history, stories, legends, etc, and engrained rituals that have evolved over time.

Positive Views on Model	Negative Views on Model
• Identifies the core elements which management can influence • Allows recognition of past in cultural development	• Culture difficult to define • More than one culture can co-exist in an organisation • Low consideration of external effects such as economy or society

47. LEWIN FORCE FIELD ANALYSIS

Lewin Force Field Analysis (1947) considers and compares the forces for and forces against a proposal, decision or project typically involving change.

Lewin Force Field Analysis (1947) looks at the forces that are at play in a change scenario. There will be forces that want the change, the pro-stakeholders, and there will be opposition forces from the stakeholders who object to the change. Lewin's model aims to assess how these forces will interact, and identify strategies for harnessing and combating the forces as necessary to secure the desired outcome.

Lewin suggested that to drive change, management needed to recognise the two perspectives, learning how to harness the positive forces to help drive the change, whilst developing strategy to deflect, mitigate or repel the negative forces.

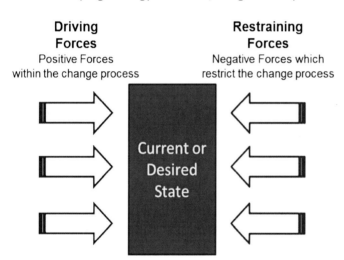

Driving Forces	Restraining Forces
Positive Forces within the change process	Negative Forces which restrict the change process

Force Field Analysis – Kurt Lewin

Positive Views on Model	Negative Views on Model
• Identifies forces for and against a project • Helps develop strategy to harness and combat forces as applicable	• Difficult to quantify forces • Forces often change without management being involved • No certainty that all forces have been included?

48. MASLOW HIERARCHY OF NEEDS

The Maslow Hierarchy of Needs pyramid examines the aspects of life that an individual seeks to gain from a work engagement, starting with basic physical and physiological needs through to aspects that make an individual feel good about themselves, referred to as Self-Actualisation.

The Maslow Hierarchy of Needs pyramid is a long established model which identifies, categorises and ranks the various aspects that an individual wants to secure from his or her work activity.

The base of the pyramid are the things that the person looks to sort out in the first instance (Physiological Needs – e.g. food and water), then those in the second tier and so on. The top of the pyramid are the highly desirable aspects that a well–rewarded and thus motivated person may cherish such as experiencing purpose, enjoying a challenge, creativity, etc.

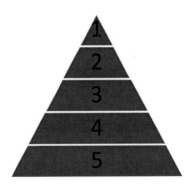

1 Self Actualisation

2 Self Esteem

3 Love & Belonging

4 Safety & Security

5 Physiological Needs

Notwithstanding this pinnacle, an individual may become despondent if there is nothing left for them to strive for. Good management will ensure that the individual always has something to aim for, a new target, a promotion, extra prestige, etc.

Positive Views on Model	Negative Views on Model
• Very well established and acknowledged concept • Clearly identifies priorities for an individual	• Different people may have a different pyramid make–up. • The pyramid can change, e.g. upon father or motherhood

49. MINTZBERG MANAGEMENT ROLES

The Mintzberg Management Rules are a list of ten rules a manager must follow in order to achieve his or her core objectives and ensure managerial success.

Mintzberg identified and categorised 10 key roles that a typical manager needs to possess in order to be effective although not all managers need to comply with all ten roles dependent upon their managerial function. These roles fall into three distinct groupings: Interpersonal, Informational and Decisional.

	Mintzberg's Role	Skill Set Required
Interpersonal	**Figurehead** Employees respect the person's authority	Reputation, assertiveness, confidence, humility and image
	Leader Manager displays leadership skills	Reputation, stature, charisma and emotional intelligence
	Liaison Manager can liaise both internally and externally	Networking, and communication skills
Informational	**Monitor** Has a good awareness of operating environment	System, industry, market and cultural knowledge
	Disseminator Can effectively communicate with the team	Information management, communication and presentation skills
	Spokesperson Is able to speak-up for the team when required	Negotiation, charisma, communication and presentation skills
Decisional	**Entrepreneur** Generates ideas, delivers change & solves issues	Vision, initiative, passion and change management skills
	Disturbance Handler Can help manage, mediate and resolve conflict	Ability to listen, empathy, compassion, focus and fairness
	Resource Allocator Can manage resources both personnel & funding	Numeric, interpersonal and analytical skills
	Negotiator Manager is able to negotiate well for the team	Ability to listen, analytical skills, determination and a win-win focus

Positive Views on Model	Negative Views on Model
• Identifies key areas in which a manager needs to perform well • Roles evolve so skills may need to be developed as well	• Roles relate to success of manager not the organisation • Ignores power or ownership as an issue

50. THEORY X, THEORY Y AND THEORY Z

Theory X, Y and Z suggest that "people" are one of three core types. Originally McGregor stated that people are either inherently lazy (Type X) or seek work as a motivating activity (Type Y). Ouchi later suggested that there was a third type, people who wanted team involvement and the relationships that this brings.

McGregor's Theory X & Theory Y assumptions suggested that employees in an organisation fell into one of two categories:

1. Employees were either inherently lazy **(Theory X)** or;
2. Employees actively looked for work as they saw it as a motivating and rewarding endeavour providing stimulus and personal gratification **(Theory Y)**.

Later, Ouchi introduced a third idea entitled "**Theory Z**" which focused attention on the needs of the team members. These included an individual's desire to be part of a group, to feel they contribute to a team activity and that they derive social benefit from the collective activity.

- People inherently dislike work and are lazy
- People must be coerced or controlled to do work to achieve objectives
- People prefer to be directed
- Motivation is achieved only through pay and basic rewards

- People view work as being as natural as play and rest, and just as enjoyable
- People will exercise self-direction and self-control towards achieving objectives they are committed to
- People learn to accept and seek responsibility
- Motivation can come from challenges, responsibility and self-esteem needs

- Aim should be for positive morale of the employee, motivation, and their general happiness
- Strive for stable employment conditions and low staff turnover
- Employer-employee contract leading to loyalty and commitment
- Produces high productivity and contribution levels

Positive Views on Model	Negative Views on Model
• Very well established and understood model	• Many consider there to be far more iterations • Model is arguably too simple

51. TUCKMAN TEAM DEVELOPMENT CYCLE

The Tuckman Team Development Cycle (1965) looks at how a team is established and the phases necessary to make the team effective. This model has been added to in recent years however the core content remains the same: FORM–STORM–NORM–PERFORM.

Tuckman suggests that first of all you need to FORM a team, let it have some time to get organised (STORM), let the organisation develop its NORMal practices, and then let the team PERFORM as it is intended.

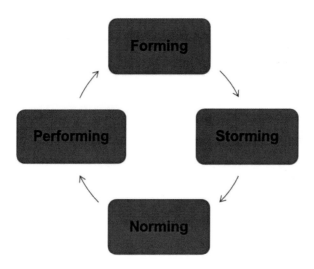

Later versions of this model in 1977 include DORMING, ADJOINING and MOURNING which reflect the fact that after performing you should reflect on the performance and adjust the team before forming again or manage its demise. These are the feedback and adjustment loops within the team development model.

Positive Views on Model	Negative Views on Model
• Helps establish where a team is in its development and what management intervention is needed.	• Only an observational model • Doesn't directly suggest remedy, direction, process or solutions

SECTION 6 // MARKET & PRICE ANALYSIS

- Porter Competitive Advantage Model
- Porter Five Force Model
- Pricing Strategies
- Supply Market Analysis

52. PORTER COMPETITIVE ADVANTAGE MODEL

The Porter Competitive Advantage Model (1980) suggests that for an organisation to succeed, it needs to have one of three core strategies: 1) Cost Leadership, 2) Differentiation of product or service, or 3) Specific Focus on some aspect often a niche or market segment.

The Porter Competitive Advantage Model examines the strategies which are most likely to be successful in a certain type of market. Porter suggested three main strategies: Cost Leadership, Differentiation or Focus. Porter's view was that organisations which did not adopt one of these, would get "stuck in the middle", unable to make optimum profits, leaving them unable to invest, and vulnerable to the pull of obscurity and decline.

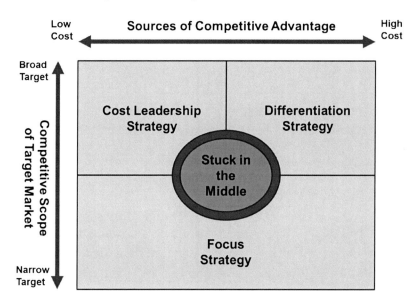

Porter identified that the choice of strategy is determined by two core factors, the competitive scope in the market and the number of sources or suppliers available.

Positive Views on Model	Negative Views on Model
• Highly reputable and long established • Lots of supporting evidence	• The three strategies are very generic • There are more core strategies and numerous iterations

53. PORTER FIVE FORCE MODEL

The Porter Five Force Model is an established model used to consider forces that affect the competitiveness of a market. These include the competition in the current market, the impact of new market entrants and alternative products, as well as pressure from buyers and suppliers.

The Porter Five Force model (1980) considers the amount of demand that may be in the existing market, and how that may be affected by:

- The rivalry of the existing companies in the market as they fight for the demand that exists;
- The impact of the customer base such as earnings, changes in taste, the economic outlook, taxation, etc;
- The pressures that a supplier can exert in the market by raising or lowering prices, or changing the supply of product into the market;
- The impact that the arrival (or departure) of a competitor has on the market and the barriers which prevent entering or leaving the market;
- The impact alternative solutions will have on demand in the market, especially if it is underpinned by legislation, cost or technology.

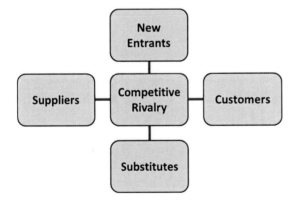

Since 1985, and the original publication, a sixth force has been identified, that of complementary products which may affect demand, for example the price of fuel in the car market.

Positive Views on Model	Negative Views on Model
- Highly reputable and long established model - Can be adapted to reflect real numbers	- Identifying the full extent of the forces can be an issue and they can change quickly. - Doesn't consider issues like geography or political pressure

54. PRICING STRATEGIES

Pricing Strategies are used within the marketing function of an organisation to strategically price items. There are many such pricing policies such as Cost–Plus Pricing, Penetration, Loss–Leaders, Market Pricing, or Skimming.

Whilst there are a huge number of pricing strategies, below are a few of the more popular options:

Cost-Plus Pricing	• Price is the cost price of the goods or services with a profit margin added on.
Market Pricing	• Price is set to reflect the price levels in the market or that a customer will pay.
Market Penetration	• Price is set to below the prevailing market rate to gain market share.
Skimming	• High price set to gain high profit per unit during launch phase to recoup development costs.
Psychological Pricing	• Price is set just below psychological barriers typically of the form $19.99.
Value Based Pricing	• Price is calculated around the perceived value that the product gives the consumer.
Loss Leader	• Supplier sells below cost to generate market share to capture a competitive advantage.
Predatory Pricing	• Similar to Loss-Leader, but price is set very low (though not lossmaking) to poach business.

Understanding the structure and positioning of a price can help identify the short, medium and long term strategy an organisation is trying to adopt. Use of the wrong mechanism can lead to risk of losses, higher levels of inventory, heavy discounting or shortages in production capacity amongst others.

Positive Views on Model	Negative Views on Model
• Helps unite operational and commercial strategies • Many pricing strategies are proven to be effective	• There are perhaps too many options to choose from • Strategies are often modified and implemented without trial

55. SUPPLY MARKET ANALYSIS

Supply Market Analysis is used to position suppliers in the market relative to their cost and quality. This is useful when examining an organisation and it supports the formation or analysis of a supplier strategy.

The Supply Market Analysis can be used to help position suppliers in their market based on their relative quality and cost offerings. It helps ensure that the product mix of an organisation covers the intended client base, budget or quality aspiration, and can prevent different brands from competing unnecessarily amongst themselves. Quality is however very subjective, so endeavour to use multiple opinions to reduce "Group Think" – consider the example below.

Considering the mix of products a supplier has can reveal the supplier's strategy, although some organisations actively allow their relative brands to operate in an autonomous way without cross fertilisation of ideas or strategy, perceiving internal competition to be both healthy and beneficial.

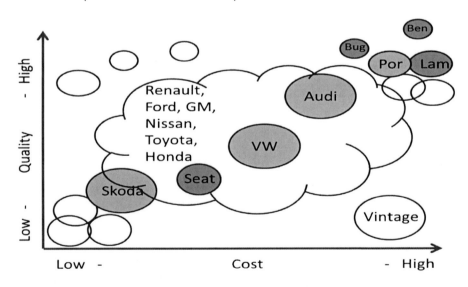

Positive Views on Model	Negative Views on Model
• Clearly shows product and market strategy when applied • Helps understand how segment coverage is developing	• What is shown may not be what the company intended • Definition of quality can be very subjective

Section 7 // Marketing

- Ansoff Matrix
- Boston Consulting Group Matrix
- Kotler 4P Model
- Product Life Cycle

56. ANSOFF MATRIX

The Ansoff Matrix is used to identify the best method to adopt when planning to develop the business coverage of an organisation especially with new products or in new markets.

The Ansoff Matrix (1957) is a standard four box matrix used to determine the best strategy for the development of an organisation's product and market strategy. The model identifies four routes to generating business expansion:

Market Development – Uses existing products in new markets.
Market Penetration – Sell more of existing product into existing markets.
Product Development – Introduce new products into existing markets.
Diversification – Market and launch new products into new markets.

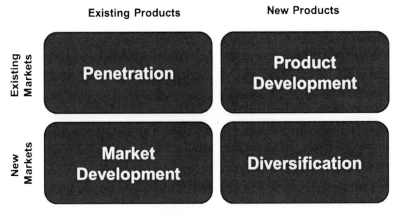

The four approaches were originally intended to grow the sales volume in the organisation, however the four strategies can equally as well be used to enable the organisation to target higher margin opportunities or customers with a lower risk profile.

Positive Views on Model	Negative Views on Model
• Clearly identifies marketing and product option • Helps plan product diversity and portfolio planning especially if used with Boston Consulting Group Matrix – See Model 57	• Applicable in commercial and FMCG businesses, but limited benefit in Public Sector or charities • Doesn't include the dynamics and nature of the market

57. Boston Consulting Group Matrix

The Boston Consulting Group Matrix is used to identify and categorise products within a corporate product portfolio recognising products in the portfolio evolve over time. Product categories in this model are: "Question Marks, "Stars", "Cash Cows" and "Dogs".

The Boston Consulting Group Matrix (1984) is used to categorise products within an organisation's portfolio which are developing or fading.

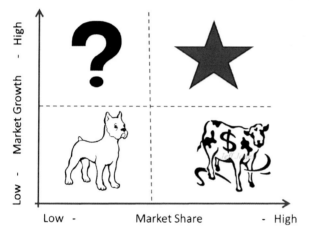

Question Marks are new products, perhaps from the R&D department, in their infancy; it is uncertain as to whether these will be a success or not. Some will fail others will become Stars and will form the new flagship products for the company. Money is spent to launch and publicise these new products, however, in time the product will wane, and marketing funds will cease, as the company seeks to gain as much revenue as possible, these are then referred to as Cash Cows. Inevitably over time the Cash Cows will themselves start to wilt and become Dog products. These may be disposed of or in some cases the product may be re-energised with a marketing regime, it may become fashionable, be labelled "retro", vintage or antique, etc.

Positive Views on Model	Negative Views on Model
• Helps identify a proactive product strategy • Helps highlight the need for product innovation and design	• Fails to drive marketing or spend decisions • Only focuses on market share and growth

58. KOTLER 4P MODEL

The Kotler 4P Model is a classic marketing model used at the customer end of the Supply Chain to identify the core ingredients of a correctly marketed product. It should consider the needs and features of the <u>Product</u>, make sure the <u>Price</u> is competitive, in a clear market <u>Place</u>, underpinned with an effective <u>Promotion</u> strategy.

The Kotler 4P Model identifies the four key considerations when marketing a product in a market, and whilst modern Supply Chain philosophy promotes the use of *Pull* production – i.e. product is only made once a customer has placed a demand – some Supply Chains, particularly in retail, still need to consider the concept of a traditional marketing approach.

The **Product** needs to be something that the customers in the market want, it must be positioned at a **Price** that the market can accept or afford, it must be sold in the right **Place**, and have the right **Promotion** to allow would–be customers to identify with it.

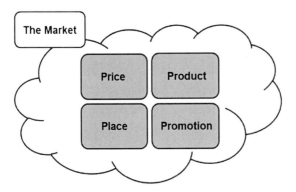

Failure to get the marketing right, and the organisation faces losses related to lost investment and potentially excess inventory, as well as opportunity losses as it could have been undertaking other profitable activities instead.

Positive Views on Model	Negative Views on Model
• Simple and established concept • Works well in FMCG and well established markets • Good in markets where price is a dominant factor	• A PUSH not a PULL strategy • Low consideration of demand levels in the market • Poor with bespoke products or services

59. PRODUCT LIFE CYCLE

A Product's Life Cycle is its journey from conception through to its ultimate demise. The cycle has four distinct phases – Introduction, Growth, Maturity and Decline – and organisational strategy needs to reflect this.

The Product Life Cycle attributed to Theodore Levitt (1965) helps management plan strategy both in terms of sales and investment. The Product Life Cycle Model is useful to understand where a product sits within its lifecycle curve, and the necessary actions or investment required to optimise its impact.

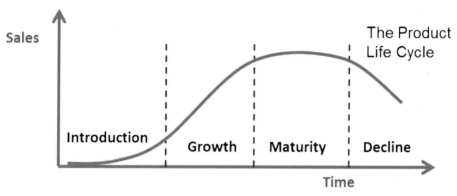

The curve reflects changes in demand over the course of a product's operational life with the four phases aligning with the boxes in the Boston Consulting Group Matrix. For each a distinct strategy should be adopted. During the Introduction Phase somewhat high levels of investment are needed to promote the product with Return On Investment (ROI) relatively low. In the Growth Phase investment is maintained, the product sales start to repay the effort and investment. At Maturity, the need for marketing reduces and high levels of sales and profit should be forthcoming. During the Decline Phase no investment should be undertaken as demand is waning, with efforts made to extend the product life.

Positive Views on Model	Negative Views on Model
• Clear model in many instances • Ties in well with the Boston Consulting Group Matrix four quadrants	• Gives few ideas on strategy • Curve may have fluctuations driven by climate, fashion, economic aspects, etc

SECTION 8 // PROCUREMENT

- Activity Based Costing
- Bartolini Scorecard
- Carter 9C Model
- Crocker Simplified Service Gap Model
- Five Rights of Purchasing
- Kraljic Matrix
- Maturity Assessment Model
- Monczka MSU Model
- O'Brien 5i Model
- POD Procurement
- Steele & Court Supplier Preferencing Model
- Syson Positioning Graph – Strategic Policies
- Syson Positioning Graph – Strategic Performance
- Total Cost of Ownership Model
- Value Analysis & Value Stream Mapping

60. ACTIVITY BASED COSTING

Activity Based Costing looks at how cost can be allocated within a business based on usage or some other activity. When implemented, this gives a fairer, more strategic and manageable allocation of cost across a business.

The concept of Activity Based Costing (ABC) has evolved over the years to enable organisations to allocate costs more strategically within business units, through geographic locations, by product or simply by usage. This concept is liked by accountants and managers who feel they do not get value for money from corporate overheads, and has developed significantly since usage data has become easier and cheaper to track using IT solutions along with data capture from advances like swipe cards, coded access on equipment such as photocopiers, or vehicle tracking systems amongst others. Allocation can be via a number of options including:

*   **Equitable Allocation** – Cost is distributed equally across the stakeholder groups irrespective of usage. Easy to calculate but penalises those who do not use the goods or services.
*   **Allocation by usage** – Cost is allocated pro rata to usage, however it can be difficult and costly to directly attribute usage, and can result in internal conflict between departments.
*   **Allocation by sales** – Cost is allocated to department in relation to the level of sales contributed. Assumes that a department with a large sales contribution will have a corresponding ability to contribute.
*   **Allocation by Geography** – Cost is allocated based on geography, i.e. if the cost was consumed in Italy it would be allocated to the Italian business, etc. Can cause national or regional resentment and increases risk of exploitation of different tax regimes.
*   **Allocation by Product** – Cost is allocated based on the product within the organisation's portfolio to which it relates.

Positive Views on Model	Negative Views on Model
• Improves management of costs • Increases visibility and ownership • Brings budget and behaviour closer together	• Data capture can be an issue • Selection of the allocation method can cause problems • Workers start to hide usage

61. BARTOLINI SCORECARD

The Bartolini Scorecard is used in Category Management to evaluate the suitability and potential viability of a procurement category, enabling categories to be prioritised and resources allocated within set up process.

Using a structured questionnaire, the Bartolini scorecard collects relevant data pertaining to a category, evaluates its potential and scores the category accordingly. This detail can then be used to 1) prioritise categories, 2) allocate resources including finance, personnel and time allocation, and 3) identify commercial potential from the category.

The model identifies 5 categories against which it evaluates the category, these are:

i.   **Category specific issues** – Aspects relating to the goods and services or collective product segment, for example complexity of the product or lead–time for delivery.
ii. **Procurement facets** – Consideration of the procurement process, risk analysis, desired outcomes, specifications, stakeholders, etc.
iii. **Internal and organisational facets** – The structure of the organisation, for example its history, geography, management hierarchy, culture, stakeholder engagement and expectations.
iv. **Market facets** – Based on the Porter Five Force model, this looks at forces and dynamics in the market, buyers, sellers, barriers to entry, new entrants and alternative solutions.
v.   **Supplier facets** – Finally the model looks at the supplier base, considering aspects such as its competitive nature, prevailing margins, perceived saving opportunity, as well as the type of suppliers, their organisational structure, whether the product is bespoke or generic, design and specification commitment, volume, and spend potential.

Positive Views on Model	Negative Views on Model
• Structured method of evaluation against a clear criteria • Enables supplier comparison • Enables resource allocation	• Fixed evaluation criteria • One of several similar models in existence

62. Carter 9C Model

The Carter 9C Model is an internationally renowned model that is used to assess suppliers prior to contract award, and can be used thereafter to assess supplier performance once service is underway.

The Carter 9C Model is a highly recognised model for the assessment of potential suppliers in a tender situation. The model incorporates weighting to allow the assessment to accurately balance the importance of the factors being measured with the quality of the evidence used to underpin the analysis. The Cs of each measured facet are as follows:

Capacity	Has the supplier got the physical resources to deliver the requirement
Consistency	Can the supplier deliver the requirement to a consistent specification and quality
Culture	Will the suppliers core values be compatible with ours
Cash	Has the supplier got a sufficient level of financial means to fulfil its obligations
Cost	Are the goods or services offered at a competitive cost
Control of Process	Has the management at the supplier got control of its process
Competency	Does the supplier employ competent personnel and systems
Commitment to Quality	Does the supplier have a focus on quality and quality management
Clean	Is the supplier ethical, responsible and free of corruption

Each contractor is measured based on the agreed weighting and reflecting the quality of the evidence. The scores are then multiplied together to generate an overall score for the potential supplier.

Positive Views on Model	Negative Views on Model
• Reflects critical areas of supplier analysis • Enables evidence and risk to be incorporated into the analysis • Facilitates weighting of facets	• Debate on the number (7,8,9 or 10) of Cs • No clear definition of some of the Cs, e.g. Communication, Customer, CSR, Compliance

63. Crocker Simplified Service Gap Model

The Crocker Simplified Service Gap Model looks at the causes of gaps in services provision between customer expectations, actual service delivery and the customer perception of the service experience.

Understanding the causes of customer dissatisfaction is essential to an organisation and its ability to gain and maintain customers over a sustained period. The Crocker Simplified Service Gap Model looks at two distinct gaps within the service provision that generate the mismatch between service expectation and service perception.

SIMPLIFIED GAP MODEL

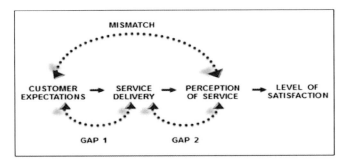

REASONS FOR GAPS

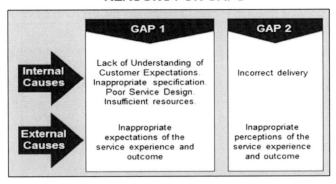

Once the gaps have been identified quality improvement solutions can be implemented to meet the customer expectations.

Positive Views on Model	Negative Views on Model
• Clearly shows where the service fails	• Assumes no third party interference in the delivery

64. Five Rights of Purchasing

The Five Rights of Purchasing concept is a core element of effective procurement. The Five Rights clarify what the buyer is entitled to expect when signing a contract or placing a purchase order.

The Five Rights of Purchasing highlight very succinctly what the buyer should anticipate when agreeing a deal with a supplier.

Right Quality	•The **Right Quality**: Conforming to the specification' and 'fitness for purpose', the costs of getting quality wrong, specifications and quality, approaches to managing supplier quality
Right Quantity	•The **Right Quantity**: determining the quantity required, factors influencing the choice of how much to buy, minimum order levels and values
Right Place	•The **Right Place**: in bound transportation of goods to the delivery point, issues arising from international transportation
Right Time	•The **Right Time**: internal, external and total lead time and factors that influence lead time, expediting, measuring supplier delivery performance
Right Price	•The **Right Price**: the different types of cost, and where purchase price fits in, factors affecting how a supplier prices their products or services

It is not unreasonable that the buyer receives goods or services which meet the specification and are of the Right Quality, that these are supplied in the Right Quantity required and stated on the purchase order, and delivered to the Right Place as indicated. This delivery should also occur at the Right Time stated or within a reasonable time commensurate with the prevailing circumstances, and should be at an agreed Right Price. This price should be a total price including delivery, and any extras.

Positive Views on Model	Negative Views on Model
• Helps a buyer determine if they have been fairly treated • Clearly identifies what a buyer can expect from a supplier	• Does not address a bad decision nor eliminate poor value for money or an inappropriate specification

65. KRALJIC MATRIX

The Kraljic Matrix is an internationally recognised four box model which analyses the interrelation (from the buyer's perspective) between value and risk, although a number of variants do exist. Each box refers to a type of relationship, these being: Strategic, Bottleneck, Non-Critical and Leverage.

The Kraljic Matrix (1983) examines the relationship between value and risk although some texts have different axis titles. An organisation may use this as part of its segmentation process to position contracts or procurement relationships. The model helps identify strategic characteristics of an item, for example, a bottleneck item which would need special consideration as the buying relationship would be restrictive.

Note: Consider these perspectives in conjunction with the Steele & Court "Supplier Preferencing Model" (See Model 70) as it needs to tie in with the supplier's perspective – you may deem a facet of your procurement to be mission critical but the supplier may see you as a nuisance and have no motivation to form a relationship between the two organisations.

Positive Views on Model	Negative Views on Model
• Very commonly used and recognised model • Simple and clear matrix	• Lots of different variants • Cost not considered directly in the model • Can lack precision

66. MATURITY ASSESSMENT MODEL

The Maturity Assessment Model was developed to provide a collaborative profile for an organisation. It provides a benchmark and development profile to be used for internal assessment for the buying organisation or as an initial profile of potential collaborative partners.

The Maturity Assessment Model assesses three key variables: **Attributes**, **Abilities** and **Attitudes**, with the target being an optimum score of four in each, representing an effective and integrated collaboration.

Maturity Assessment

	Attributes	Ability	Attitude
The maturity matrix provides a platform against which organisations can review their internal development needs.			
A	Operational processes are well defined and integrate collaborative approaches	There is a high level of experience at all levels focused on effective collaboration	There is clear corporate commitment and leadership that cascades throughout the operations
B	There is limited application of shared processes and performance indicators	There are individuals at various levels that have demonstrable skills in collaboration	There is evidence of successful individual collaborative programmes in effect
C	There are robust internal processes and performance indicators	There is appreciation of collaborative approaches but a lack of skills	There is appreciation at the operating level of the value of effective relationships
D	Operates with a traditional contract and procedural based approach	No appreciation of a practical approach to the value of relationships	Only operates a robust and effective arms length contracting approach

Accordingly it is an important tool to be used when implementing BS11000 the standard for Collaborative Business Relationships. A note of caution however, it is vital to ensure consistency and objectivity when scoring in order to provide a factual and accurate view of the relationship.

Positive Views on Model	Negative Views on Model
• Gives consistent framework for Buyer assessment • Good for consistency and audit	• Assessment might be subjective which would undermine the results

67. MONCZKA MSU MODEL

The Monczka MSU Model is a systematic process which analyses each step in the procurement process with the aim of improving the strategic procurement performance, efficiency and effectiveness of the organisation.

The model was conceived at Michigan State University by Dr Robert Monczka (can be called the MSU Model) and often compared with Kraljic. It systematically addresses each stage of the organisation's procurement process. As each step is considered, it is analysed, audited and mapped to give a clear understanding of its objective. Monczka suggested that there are 8 different strategic processes which can be seen, these are:

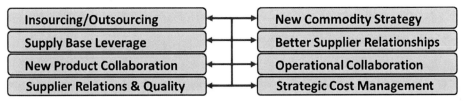

1. **Insourcing/Outsourcing** – Is the activity a core competency of the organisation?
2. **Development of commodity strategies** – Do the commodities have specific needs or requirements?
3. **Leverage of a world class supply base** – Is the supply base effective, best of breed, challenged and stretched?
4. **Development and management of supplier relationships** – Are win-win, trusting relationships in place with the core suppliers?
5. **Supplier collaboration with new product development** – Is there Early Supplier Involvement (ESI) in the R&D or marketing teams?
6. **Supplier collaboration in operation and final delivery process** – Are suppliers involved in the whole supply chain with ESI, VMI, etc?
7. **Quality and supplier development** – Is there dialogue with suppliers over quality and performance improvements?
8. **Strategic cost management** – Are costs managed and appropriate across the Supply Chain, are cost reduction processes in place?

Positive Views on Model	Negative Views on Model
• A systematic, analytical and structured model • Based on best practice	• May not apply to all organisations, for example the public sector

68. O'BRIEN 5I MODEL

The O'Brien 5i Model is a five stage (5i) model designed to help create and maintain a category management system. The model looks at the process from kick off (Initiation) through to the realisation of benefits (Improvement).

The O'Brien 5i Model is delivered using a series of workshops which generate a logical transition through the preparation and management of an effective category management solution irrespective of the commodity or products involved. Each workshop has a specific objective, is structured and has specific attendees to ensure appropriate stakeholders are involved throughout the formation of the category structure. The steps are as follows:

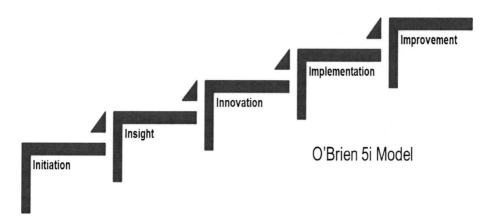

O'Brien 5i Model

Initiation: Kick–Off workshop. Outline the objectives and setting the rules
Insight: Situation Analysis workshop. Identify product/company needs
Innovation: Strategic Options workshop. Looks at possible solutions
Implementation: Implementation workshop. Make the changes
Improvement: Improvement workshop. Realise the benefits and tweak

Also consider other similar models which include: CIPS Cat Management Model, AT Kearney 7 Step model and the Partnering Group 8 Step Model.

Positive Views on Model	Negative Views on Model
• Well established Category Management model • Structured and easy to use	• A number of different alternative models exist and can get muddled

69. POD Procurement Model

The POD Procurement Model is designed to overcome barriers when looking to create collaborative commercial agreements. The model uses mathematical algorithms that increase both buyer savings and supplier profits by focusing suppliers away from contract value and onto reducing cost whilst focussing the buyer on collaboration and shared goals.

The POD Model is a mathematical calculation inserted into standard commercial agreements without creating a direct impact or altering the pre–existing terms and conditions. The mathematical algorithms can be used as an integral part of a standard contract enabling both parties to utilise any/all of the benefits therein, without invoking a contract re-negotiation.

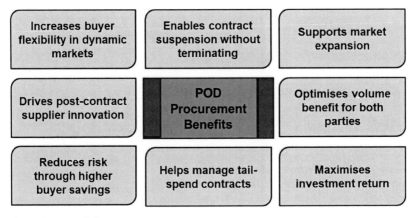

The POD Model:
- Can be used in most commercial agreements where the buyer has committed to procuring goods/ services
- Requires no new tools or technology
- No additional contract negotiation required
- No increase of buyer or supplier workloads, business costs or risks
- Does not replace or remove the right to re–negotiate a contract

Positive Views on Model	Negative Views on Model
• A scalable solution for collaboration • Delivers mutual financial benefit without increasing buyer or supplier risk	• Requires a change in organisational culture • Challenges traditional contracting models

70. Steele & Court Supplier Preferencing Model

The Steele & Court (1996) Supplier Preferencing Model is used to examine the view a supplier may have of a customer. This is often utilised by the customer to understand how valued its business is to a supplier or to evaluate what strategy the supplier has adopted towards it.

Whilst the Kraljic Model (See Model 65) is useful for understanding the prevailing risk and reward dynamic in relation to a supplier, it is not unreasonable to suppose that a supplier would have a similar view of the buying organisation. The Steele & Court (1996) Supplier Preferencing Model in a contract setting is useful for assessing what this perspective may be and helps when determining the strategy taken by the suppliers to an organisation, be they a nonchalant supplier, or indeed a supplier for whom your organisation is seen as core.

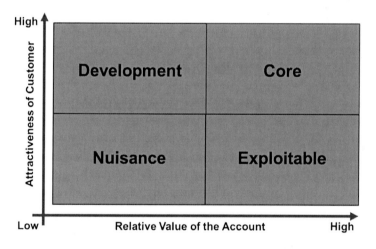

Understanding these different perspectives is important. A supplier perceiving *you* as a "Nuisance" customer will have a very different approach than one who sees *you* as "Core". This can lead to issues where the different parties have a conflicting view or allow commercial opportunities to be missed. Note parallels with Kraljic (Model 65) which looks at the Buyer's view of the Supplier.

Positive Views on Model	Negative Views on Model
• Well known and understood four box model • Simple to apply and understand	• No specific direction on remedial actions

71. Syson Positioning Graph – Strategic Policies

The Syson Positioning Model illustrates the relationship between the Procurement activity and its evolution from an efficient transactional activity through to a proactive, effective function within the organisation.

Syson saw the Procurement function divided into three main areas of focus: transaction, commercial and proactive. The more developed the Procurement activity, the greater its involvement in commercial and strategic activities and the more involved Procurement becomes in commercial and strategic activities the greater its return of investment.

Positioning Graph = Strategies / Policies

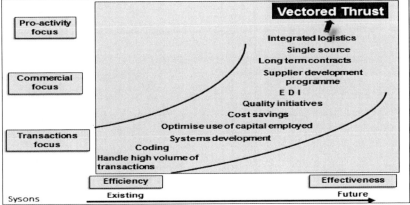

(Source: Cited in Bailey, P., Farmer, D., Crocker, B. et al. (2008). *Procurement, Principles and Management*)

Syson viewed that Procurement has been transformed from a service function with aims expressed by price, quality and delivery to one which makes a contribution to sustainable competitive advantage by reducing the cost of ownership, cycle time reduction and improving time to market, moving from being efficient to being effective and aiming for proactivity.

Positive Views on Model	Negative Views on Model
• Provides useful Procurement road–map or pathway • Highlights ideas and opportunities	• Lacks detail as to how this may be achieved

71A. Syson Positioning Graph – Strategic Performance

The Syson Model, in addition to highlighting the various activities, strategies and directions that a procurement function should endeavour to embrace, highlights the various measures of performance that should be introduced to measure and manage the transitional activity.

The Syson Strategies and Policies detailed in Model 71 were assigned to individual KPI indicators and measurement criteria to ensure that each aspect was driven forward to generate the best commercial return from the developing operational activity resulting in the Syson Measures of Performance Graph as shown below:

Positioning Graph- Measures of Performance

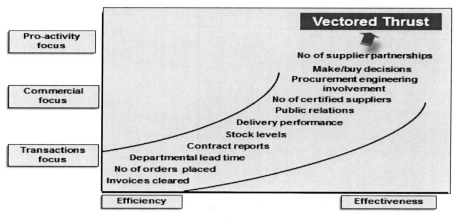

Whilst a subset of the main Syson Model, this secondary element highlights the aspects of a business that can benefit from the Syson transition, each with demonstrable benefit and clear metrics for the organisation to assess and manage development against.

Positive Views on Model	Negative Views on Model
• Highlights clear operational benefits • Introduces a measure or KPI against each operational opportunity	• The KPI measures are only a suggested few with many others existing • KPI measures address generic rather than bespoke opportunities

72. TOTAL COST OF OWNERSHIP MODEL

The Total Cost of Ownership Model considers all the costs associated with a purchase as opposed to just the purchase price. This gives a far better reflection of what a purchase may cost in totality over its operational life.

The Total Cost of Ownership Model identifies the core elements of costs to be considered when determining the "best solution". It's not just the invoice price, but the pre-purchase research, the preparation of the business case, the tender process, the meetings, the pre-purchase dialogue, etc, as well as the after costs associated with the purchase, such as the maintenance, upgrades, repairs, durables, training, security, product support, technical backup, etc. This can be seen illustrated by the Total Cost Iceberg (Crocker & Jessop) below.

The Price-Total Cost of Ownership Iceberg

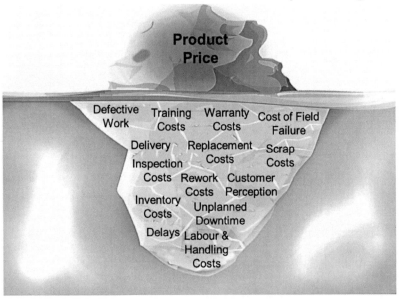

Positive Views on Model	Negative Views on Model
• Clearly illustrates all the costs that make up the Total Cost • Iceberg analogue easy to understand and associate with	• Needs knowledgeable user to be able to recognise all the associated costs even non-recurring or one-off costs

73. VALUE ANALYSIS & VALUE STREAM MAPPING

Value Analysis is a structured process that aims to ensure the production process delivers all the elements of the specification and aspirations of the Stakeholders at the lowest Total Cost of Ownership. Value Stream mapping identifies where in the process the Value is generated.

The concept of Value Analysis is often introduced as a process which looks to understand the costs involved with a production process, stripping out any cost which does not add value within the overall production schemes; if it doesn't add positively to the end goal, the final solution, and can be removed without detriment, it is removed. The removal must not restrict performance, damage quality, or in any way reduce the benefit to the user.

In contrast Value Stream Mapping looks at where in a process value is added. It looks at how effort, time and process change the total value of the components into something of greater worth.

As an example, consider a block of stone. A sculptor starts chipping, each hammer blow creates value as the rock becomes a work of art, the final piece being more valuable than the original block. Once formed in outline, the sculptor will smooth, buff and polish – all processes adding demonstrable value – until the final piece is completed. Each step can be shown within the Value Analysis to have added value, what needs to be determined is that the costs associated with each step do not outweigh the value associated with it.

Questions that are raised in Value Analysis are typically: Can this be done cheaper? Can lower cost materials be used? If lower grade materials are used, how is quality affected, does the quantity of scrap (and thus cost) increase? Is the cost and grade of the labour optimum? Can the speed of the process be improved? Should we buy or make components? And so on.

Positive Views on Model	Negative Views on Model
• Structured, systematic approach to assessing value and cost • Commonly used model to challenge processes	• Value Analysis, Value Engineering and Value Mapping are often confused • Time-consuming process

Section 9 // Quality

- 5 Whys
- Cost of Poor Quality (COPQ) Model
- Deming / Shewhart Plan–Do–Check–Act (PDCA)
- EFQM Excellence Model
- Fishbone / Root Cause Analysis / Ishikawa Diagram
- Iron Triangle Model
- Kaizen
- Ohno Seven Wastes
- Quality Circles
- Six Sigma, DMAIC and SIPOC Models
- Toyota 3M Model
- Voice of the Customer

74. 5 WHYS

The "5 Whys" concept is used to identify the root cause of a problem by repeatedly asking the question "Why?" to drill down through the surface layers of an issue to identify the real root cause.

The "5 Whys" approach, like the Ishikawa Fishbone concept, enables the user to focus on the true root cause of a problem in order to help enable remediation of the process. It is commonly used with Six Sigma activities and by organisations such as Toyota and Motorola.

The "5 Whys" concept centres around asking the question "Why" over and over again. It is asked, firstly of the issue, and then subsequently of the answers, peeling away the layers until the true root cause of the issue is identified. Assumption should however be avoided at all costs, as this can often mask key factors associated with locating the cause.

Critical to the success is the use of experienced and knowledgeable personnel – normally those in or near the process in question – and the use of observable facts associated with the problem in question. Use of normal evaluation and discursive techniques such as brainstorming, workshops, cross functional teams, supplier involvement, desk top studies, modelling, etc will all help establish a plausible answer.

Once the root cause has been identified, remedial actions can be planned and implemented. Use of the "5 Whys" technique is often engaging to personnel due to its simplicity and clear outputs.

Positive Views on Model	Negative Views on Model
• Simple to use and understand • Reduces the need to analyse statistics or data • Good with stable or moderate issues	• Needs well–informed workers • Used to shortcut analysis • Can lead to patch solutions not real remedy • Different users may give different answers

75. Cost of Poor Quality (COPQ) Model

The Cost of Poor Quality Model is a standard operations management measure and an integral part of the Six Sigma analysis; it evaluates the effective total cost and impact of a quality issue on the organisation's performance.

The Cost of Poor Quality Model is used to identify the total cost and implication associated with a quality failure. The concept is used to justify the investment in quality and support the preparation of a realistic business case underpinned with a quantifiable benefit.

Calculating the COPQ requires a broad assessment of the repercussions associated with a quality issue, these may include:

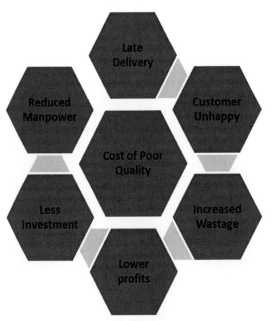

- Lost Sales & Profit
- Supplier Relationship
- Reputation Loss
- Defects
- Motivation
- Disputes
- Waste Materials
- Downtime
- Customer Delays
- Inspection Costs
- Rework
- Warranty

Positive Views on Model	Negative Views on Model
• Highlights the positive implications of managing quality • Considers total cost as opposed to issues like customer perception and PR	• No direct measurement of cost • Does not directly suggest how remediation should be undertaken

76. Deming/Shewhart Plan–Do–Check–Act (PDCA)

The Shewhart Plan–Do–Check–Act (PDCA) process is a fundamental part of a Total Quality Management (TQM) approach popularised by Deming and an integrated part of the Six Sigma concept. It ensures a structured and systematic approach to making process and quality improvements.

The Deming/Shewhart Plan–Do–Check–Act process (sometimes referred to as a wheel or cycle) is commonly adopted by businesses looking to implement and control change in processes to improve quality or efficiency.

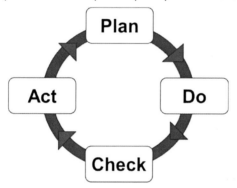

The **Plan** action assesses a problem, finds the root cause and identifies the outputs that are required from the process.

The **Do** action is responsible for implementing the Plan.

The **Check** action verifies the change, compares actual with projected results and ensures that the change has been successful.

The **Act** action addresses any issues or deviations identified by the Check action to enable the process change to be adopted.

Note: Sometimes this model is distorted for example Act can be Adjust, Plan can be Prepare, Do can be Deliver, and in some variations there is a preceding O for observation.

Positive Views on Model	Negative Views on Model
• Strong, well–used model • Works well with Continuous Improvement, and with radical or incremental change	• Needs management support • Maybe viewed as a statistical model which can alienate some users

77. EFQM Excellence Model

The EFQM Excellence Model is a quality management model developed by the European Foundation for Quality Management and is used to benchmark the proficiency and quality of an organisation based against a clear and recognised set of metrics.

The objective of the EFQM organisation is to drive quality improvements through rigorous and regular assessment based upon the model and its concepts. The model uses a systematic assessment audit, enabling clear identification of areas for improvement and focuses on eight areas of corporate excellence.

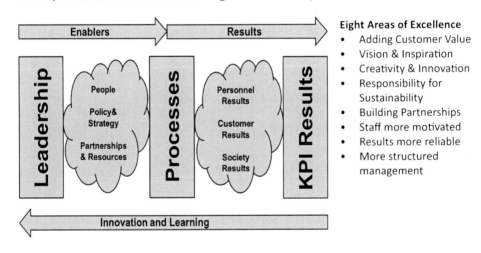

Eight Areas of Excellence
- Adding Customer Value
- Vision & Inspiration
- Creativity & Innovation
- Responsibility for Sustainability
- Building Partnerships
- Staff more motivated
- Results more reliable
- More structured management

Much of the process analysis, data collection and performance reviews are undertaken by internal operatives through self-assessment and peer observation enabling the organisation to operate and police the process using internal resources. Using internal operatives enables a higher degree of ownership, and helps buy-in when issues need resolving, giving more effective and innovative solutions and improved team understanding.

Positive Views on Model	Negative Views on Model
• Customer and objective driven • Drives continuous improvement • Sets standards and manages corporate targets	• Self-assessment needs to be carefully monitored • Prone to manipulation of findings and outputs

78. Fishbone/Root Cause Analysis/Ishikawa Diagram

The Fishbone or Ishikawa Diagram (1960) is used to breakdown an issue into its component parts to allow identification of the possible root causes of the issue thereafter assisting in the generation of a solution. Issue is traditionally quality related, but may be any problem identified.

The Fishbone or Ishikawa diagram breaks an issue – for example a quality issue – into its core components allowing an easier identification of the root cause of the problem and possible solutions. When conceived, the model had four core bones, however it has evolved into six categories (or 6Ms) in the modern Fishbone diagram, these are: Machinery, Man, Method, Mother Nature, Measurement and Materials. The example below suggests reasons why a café has started to produce cold coffee:

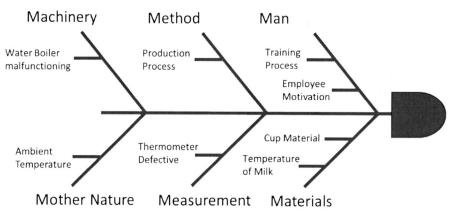

The six categories cover every element that could be present, the Mother Nature bone capturing nature, climate and *Force Majeure* aspects that were hitherto difficult to categorise. Once the possibilities have been identified, cross-functional brainstorming is used to subdivide ideas ready to be verified or eliminated as root-causes of the issue in question.

Positive Views on Model	Negative Views on Model
• Good for breaking issues into possible root-causes • Enables a possible cause to be broken down further to better identify the cause	• Needs effective cross-functional brainstorming • Can produce too many options which take time and money to evaluate/eliminate

79. Iron Triangle Model

The Iron Triangle Model looks at the relationship between Quality, Time and Cost in a project or contract activity. It is a triple constraint model, with each of the three dynamics – Quality (Specification), Time and Cost – interdependent with a change in one having a consequential change on at least one of the others.

The Iron Triangle Model considers the relationship between Quality, (Specification), Time and Cost (although it has been used in a number of other scenarios most notably political structures) and recognises that the three dynamics directly impact on the others in a project or contract activity.

For example, in a contract, the delivery of the desired Scope or Specification could be done "faster", however there would be a consequential impact with either the Cost rising (perhaps due to overtime being required) or a drop in Quality levels as the production had been rushed. Similarly, if Quality needs to be improved, invariably Cost will rise, it will take longer, or the specification will not be as good. The Iron triangle merely aims to highlight this inter-relation.

Positive Views on Model	Negative Views on Model
• Easy to understand dynamic to highlight the symbiotic relationships and inter-dependency	• Purely an illustrative model with no demonstrable outcomes.

80. KAIZEN

Kaizen is a Japanese philosophy usually associated with Toyota where continuous improvement and positive proactive change is encouraged to address issues identified by the workforce within the organisation.

Kaizen was introduced into Japan after the 1950s by Deming during the reconstruction of the Japanese economy, and was embraced by the organisations and people involved, most notably Toyota.

The concept of Kaizen is to introduce positive, proactive change in a structured and stable manner, driven from within by the workforce, with the change taking manageable, often small steps to avoid major upheaval and to ensure cross functional buy-in and support. Core to the concept is the need for continuous change driven by the internal stakeholders; the underpinning philosophy of Kaizen is that perfection is a utopia which should be aimed for, but that opportunities to improve will always be present.

Kaizen is particularly focused on developing a smooth-running, stable structure, minimising waste, and ensuring the highest quality of output with the lowest risk to the operation. These concepts were developed in depth by Toyota with their 3M waste concept – Mura, Muri & Muda – i.e. No waste, smooth flow without irregularities (see model 84). A focus on elimination of waste and improvement in Quality (the wrong quality being seen as a waste, noting over-engineering or excessively high quality for which the producer is not paid is also a waste) within every activity is a clear objective, with use of aspects such as Quality Circles, Voice of the Customer, Six Sigma, Just in Time (JIT), Kanbans, automation and other techniques to identify opportunities.

Wider, the implementation of Kaizen is often undertaken with a Plan–Do–Check–Act approach (See Model 76) to ensure a smooth, measured and calculated transition with a feedback and verification loop incorporated.

Positive Views on Model	Negative Views on Model
• Well-established and recognised approach to change • Incorporates employee buy-in	• Approach needs cross organisation commitment • Can be time-consuming

81. OHNO SEVEN WASTES

The Ohno Seven Wastes are considered the seven aspects of waste that an organisation generates in its operational activity. Ohno showed that analysing and removing these wastes would improve the efficiency, effectiveness and competitiveness of the organisation.

Originating from within the Toyota organisation and the Toyota Production System (TPS), Ohno identified seven wastes that needed to be eliminated to improve the operational excellence of the organisation. These are at the centre of the Toyota ethos on elimination of waste within their production and operation processes. The seven wastes are listed below and can be remembered by the TIMWOOD acronym:

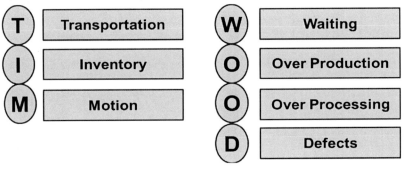

Since the publication of the Ohno Seven Wastes, there has in fact been an eighth waste added – production of an output which does not meet the customer expectations, or is not used as initially intended, or is not using all the potential of the human resource in the business.

When engaging in cost reduction activities, analysis and evaluation of each step in the operational process with these wastes in mind helps steer practitioners towards successful identification and elimination of waste.

Positive Views on Model	Negative Views on Model
• Established model highlighting possible location of waste in an organisation's delivery activities • Proven and widely utilised	• Other wastes added afterwards e.g. making something the customer rejects • Other wastes like CO_2 not included.

82. QUALITY CIRCLES

Quality Circles is a concept attributed to Deming and are small cross functional teams within the organisation which meet to discuss quality enhancement and Continuous Improvement ideas and opportunities.

The Quality Circles concept originated in the 1960s and is a powerful way of engaging staff into Quality and Continuous Improvement projects. It forms an essential part of a normal Total Quality Management process, and is commonly used within Six-Sigma projects as well, often aligned with the VOC (Voice of the Customer) approach.

The teams are cross-functional, multi-skilled and participation is often voluntary although unpaid, and not required to operate to any specific, pre-agreed format or agenda. The versatility and varied participation gives the group a broader perspective and assists the implementation of any ideas agreed and taken forward. The circles report through a supervisor into the wider organisational effort:

Positive Views on Model	Negative Views on Model
• Utilises employee expertise to improve quality and maintain Continuous Improvement	• Often needs management intervention and results can take a while to materialise

83. SIX SIGMA CONCEPT, DMAIC AND SIPOC MODELS

Six Sigma is a quality theory intended to reduce defects to less than 3.4 defects in a million units produced. The process uses statistical methods, established models and specific processes to identify where and how quality issues occur enabling their remedy. Use of SIPOC to break a Supply Chain down and the DMAIC (Define–Measure–Analyse–Improve–Control) concept to remedy issues are two such models.

The Six Sigma concept is used by organisations to drive quality processes through the organisation. It is considered by such organisations as a way of life, with process embedded in the core ethos of the management and operation.

Sceptics of Six Sigma suggest it is too heavily reliant upon statistical analysis however there are many non-mathematical concepts contained within that address organisational procedures and structure.

For example, the tool used to analyse the Supply Chain considers it over five elements as shown below and merely aims to break down the Supply Chain into manageable pieces:

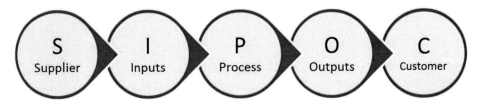

| S | I | P | O | C |
| Supplier | Inputs | Process | Outputs | Customer |

Equally, the DMAIC approach (Design–Measure–Analyse–Improve–Control) is used to create structure when addressing quality defects and reformation of the operating processes.

Positive Views on Model	Negative Views on Model
• Very structured and established approach • Underpinned with statistical data and analysis	• Mathematical and often difficult to understand • Needs trained people and be built into the culture

84. Toyota 3M Model

The Toyota 3M Model represents the three types of wastes that Toyota tries to eliminate within their operating processes: Muda (unnecessary activity in the process), Mura (irregular activity in the process), and Muri (uneven work loading in the process.

Waste management is a core part of a "Lean" and efficient organisation. The Toyota 3M Model is a core part of their waste philosophy and worth recognising. This concept forms the bedrock of all that Toyota does and stands for. Elimination of these wastes helps ensure a lean operation, reduce defects and drive quality improvements.

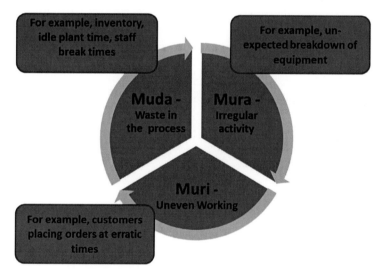

To focus the workforce and management on waste elimination, Toyota produced a list of seven key wastes or Muda which it stringently measures and relentlessly tries to eliminate. These are the Ohno Seven Wastes, see model 81.

Positive Views on Model	Negative Views on Model
• Long–established and simple model based on the successful Toyota's quality system • Drives process improvements if used within Continuous Improvement processes	• Some people struggle to recognise the quality issues in practice • Has been viewed as an automotive only model

85. VOICE OF THE CUSTOMER

The Voice of the Customer (VOC) is a simple concept within the Six–Sigma process used to understand, engage and capture ideas from both external and internal stakeholders within an organisation. These ideas help drive improvement and quality projects based on real issues.

The Voice of the Customer (VOC) process is used to encourage both internal and external "customers" to think about and document ideas that could lead to process enhancement, cost saving, waste reduction, quality improvements and other positive changes to the operation.

The VOC process is a relatively simple one; participants are asked to identify any ideas or issues which they believe would lead to a service, profit or quality improvement. Ideas are reviewed leading to a categorised set of potential improvement projects. These are then evaluated, prioritised and identified with projects often split into 1) Quick low–cost wins, 2) Low investment projects 3) Risk reduction projects and 4) Longer term ideas. Successful projects then undergo a formal project implementation process.

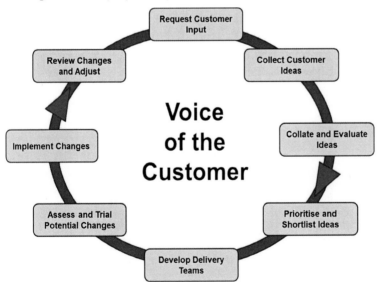

Positive Views on Model	Negative Views on Model
• Simple to implement • Engages all stakeholders	• Results can be unreliable • Takes time and investment

Section 9 // Risk

- Four T Model of Risk
- Risk-Impact Model
- Risk Types
- The Risk Cycle

86. Four T Model of Risk

The Four T Model of Risk looks at ways in which risk can be dealt with as part of the corporate strategy. The risk can be: Tolerated, Treated, Transferred or Terminated.

The Four T Model of Risk recognises that in an organisation there will be various different types of risk, and that with a limited budget and operational practicalities not all of the risks can be fully dealt with all of the time. With this understood, the Risk Manager must examine the risks, determine the impact and probability, to establish a hierarchy of risks which need to be addressed.

4T Model of Risk

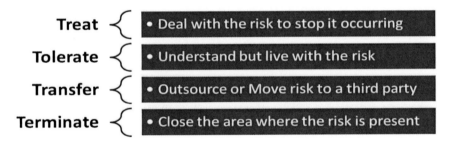

Treat — • Deal with the risk to stop it occurring

Tolerate — • Understand but live with the risk

Transfer — • Outsource or Move risk to a third party

Terminate — • Close the area where the risk is present

Once prioritised, the risk strategy can be implemented with this model suggesting four core categories of risk strategy that they will fall into and is more structured than a traditional Pareto approach where there may be a simple line drawn with risk above dealt with and risk below ignored:

Positive Views on Model	Negative Views on Model
• Clear strategy given to each identified risk • Easy to remember and apply	• May be other options or strategies to deal with the risk

87. RISK-IMPACT MODEL

The Risk-Impact Model is used to assess and categorise the severity of the risk associated with a situation based on the likely impact of the risk, and the probability that the risk may occur.

The Risk-Impact Model analyses the relationship between the probability that a risk will occur and the consequences and impact that the occurrence will cause to the organisation in question.

The probability of the risk occurring will be based on a number of different facets including statistical analysis, forecast data, historical experience and input from core stakeholders. This information generates a prediction as to how often an event will occur, enabling the organisation to decide whether remedial action is required. If remediation is undertaken the scenario is reassessed to determine the adjusted probability.

Equally important is the cost or impact an occurrence will have on an organisation, referred to in the model as "severity of impact". This may be a financial loss due to the cost of repairing the damage, the loss of sales or customers, the cost of downtime, loss of reputation etc.

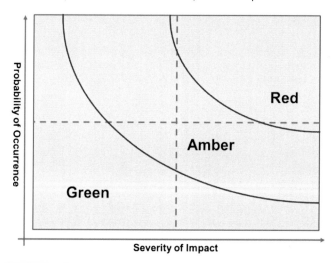

Positive Views on Model	Negative Views on Model
• Good for prioritising risk in an easy to understand format • Helps with an initial assessment of where to focus time and effort	• Doesn't identify risk, only categorises it • No real output other than a categorisation of risk

88. RISK TYPES

The concept of risk is a critical area for consideration in any successful organisation. Understanding the risks, how likely they are to occur, and what the impact will be is essential to the risk management process.

All organisations experience risk. Understanding this risk is the key to managing and mitigating the consequences and protecting the organisation from the potential issues caused by an event.

The types of risk are numerous; they can feature inside the HR function, in the finances of the organisation, within the operational activities, from the customers and suppliers, as well as from other external and internal facets of the organisation's domain.

The SWOT and STEEPLED models give some guidance to the organisation as to the source of some of the risks, however the engagement of a manager dedicated to the identification and management of risk can be invaluable.

Whilst not necessarily a model or tool, the list below helps steer attention to common types of risk that could be considered though risk is subjective and organisation specific so this is merely indicative and by no means an exhaustive list.

- Staff Risk
- Health & Safety
- Product Failure
- Contractual Risk
- Strategic Risk
- Compliance Risk
- Fraud

- Reputational Risk
- Environmental Risk
- Customer Risk
- Continuity Risk
- Supplier Risk
- Market Risk
- Logistics & Geographic Risk

Positive Views on Model	Negative Views on Model
• Highlighting different areas of risk can help steer focus	• Not really a model, just a thought provoker. • Needs underpinning with robust Risk Management

89. THE RISK CYCLE

The Risk Cycle highlights the various stages of the risk management process from identification through addressing the risk and onward monitoring. Once in process and monitored, a review of the risk remedies and the risks affecting the situation should again be assessed.

The Risk Cycle considers risk from identification through various stages to the mitigation and review. Risk is however ever-changing, so once in place and monitored the risk management solution will already be reviewing the probability of an occurrence, the impact, the success of the mitigation process, any side effects caused by the mitigation process, etc. For example, to reduce the risk of a major fire, a sprinkler system may be installed, but with this comes the risk of a false activation destroying computer equipment so are files backed-up? Fire extinguishers could be used instead but what if they are used to prop fire-doors open, etc.

Positive Views on Model	Negative Views on Model
• Structured approach to risk • Drives strategy and process	• No direct ideas, merely a process • Risk different for every organisation and structure

Section 10 // Stakeholder Management

- Egan Stakeholder Positioning Model
- Mendelow Matrix
- Stakeholder Allegiance Matrix
- Stakeholder Attitudes Model

90. Egan Stakeholder Positioning Model

The Egan Stakeholder Positioning Model is used to categorise and analyse stakeholders to enable a stakeholder strategy to be formulated to overcome issues which prevent change occurring seamlessly.

The Egan Stakeholder Positioning Model is populated with the reasons why people resist change, these include:

- **Fear of the unknown/surprise:** This occurs when change is implemented without prior warning to the affected stakeholders, and without helping them through the process;
- **Mistrust:** If a manager has not yet earned the trust of their employees, then mistrust of change will become apparent;
- **Loss of job security/control:** When companies restructure or downsize it causes fear among employees that they will lose their jobs or be moved into other positions without their consent;
- **Bad timing:** Adding too much change over a short period of time usually fails, as individuals suffer from "change fatigue";
- **An individual's predisposition toward change:** Some people dislike change because they prefer stability, becoming suspicious of change and more likely to resist.

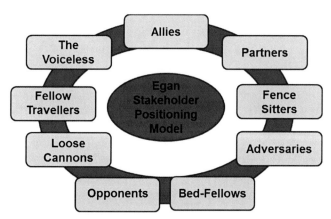

Positive Views on Model	Negative Views on Model
• Identifies the specific obstacles that need to be overcome to effect change in a project	• Does not give a remedy • Labels people which can be contentious

91. MENDELOW MATRIX

The Mendelow (1991) four box matrix helps identify the best strategy to adopt with different stakeholders based on the relative power of the stakeholder and the importance of the issue to the stakeholder.

The Mendelow (1991) Matrix combines the relative influence of stakeholders with their importance to a specific project. The matrix is used to understand the individual stakeholder needs and establish an appropriate strategy to ensure that they are managed appropriately.

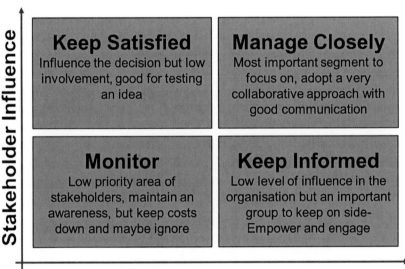

Each stakeholder type needs to be frequently reviewed throughout the project or change activity as their individuality may result in the stakeholder's needs, status, vision or perspective shifting thus requiring the strategy to be adjusted accordingly.

Positive Views on Model	Negative Views on Model
• Helps develop stakeholder specific strategy • Helps identify stakeholder risks	• Doesn't recognise changes in stakeholder perspective • May lead to stakeholders identifying others being treated differently • Variants of the box do exist

92. Stakeholder Allegiance Matrix

The Stakeholder Allegiance Matrix considers stakeholders in a project based upon their understanding of the project and their level of agreement. Determining where in the model a stakeholder sits, helps identify the strategy required to embrace, ignore or overcome them.

The Stakeholder Allegiance Matrix is a well-established positioning model to help managers understand the stance taken by different stakeholders in a project enabling strategy to be developed to manage the different factions and help ensure optimum project delivery.

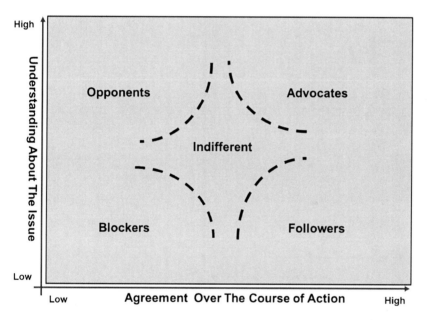

A good project manager will understand that enforcement with stakeholders is only one approach; coaching, capitulation and enticement are other possible approaches that can be used to help steer the project to a successful completion.

Positive Views on Model	Negative Views on Model
• Easy to understand positioning model • Enables clear determination of strategy in many cases	• Can pigeonhole stakeholders, and address positions with generic approaches • Labelling a group not conducive to a successful outcome

93. STAKEHOLDER ATTITUDES MODEL

The Stakeholder Attitudes Model provides some assistance in allocating a positive and appropriate response to differing attitudes in order to manage change. Stakeholders' "positioning" depends partly upon what they stand to gain or lose, coupled with education, culture and experience.

Like the Stakeholder Allegiance Matrix (see model 92), the Stakeholders Attitudes Model looks at the stakeholders and their attitude to the proposed project or business activity. It splits the stakeholders into those that are for the project and those who are against it.

Against the project	For the project
•Stands to lose from the project (reduced role, loss of job, threatens other activities); •Doesn't believe or understand Procurement, does not like outside involvement, and doesn't like change; •AIH Against it happening •LIH Lets it happen	•Stands to win from the project (e.g. will stay in a job, reduce costs, have improved position, have higher visibility); •Currently has responsibility and expertise in this area and believes in the project; •HIH Helps it happen •MIH Makes it happen

Against the Project
- Stands to Lose
- Doesn't believe or understand Purchasing
- Doesn't like you
- Doesn't like change

-ve

For the Project
- Stands to Win
- Has responsibility in the area
- Has expertise
- Believes in the Project

+ve

| **AIH** Against | **LIH** Let | **HIH** Helps | **MIH** Makes |

Positive Views on Model	Negative Views on Model
• Helps identify stakeholder positions in a project and their type of contribution	• Can pigeonhole stakeholders • Needs extra input to change or develop opinions

SECTION 11 // SUPPLY CHAIN MANAGEMENT

- Christopher & Towill Lean-Agile Matrix
- Cousins Strategic Supply Wheel
- Enterprise Resource Planning Solutions (ERP)
- Goldratt Theory of Constraints
- Incoterms
- Jackson Inventory Decision Matrix
- Lean–Agile Matrix
- Outsourcing Decision Model
- Porter Value Chain

94. CHRISTOPHER & TOWILL LEAN-AGILE MATRIX

The Christopher and Towill Lean-Agile Matrix model was developed to identify if a Lean or Agile solution should be adopted by an organisation based on its product characteristics and the demand profile for the products.

	Inventory Based Supply Chain Solution	Lean Supply
Level of Product Standardisation	**Inventory Based Supply Chain Solution** Useful where the product types tend to be generic items for example procured against a standard part number, but demand profile is uncertain	**Lean Supply** A stable demand profile and product mix leads to a focus on making product quickly to order as opposed to delivery from stock. Focus is on low or zero inventory with JIT supply of materials.
	Agile Solution Used with unpredictable demand, with products adopting bespoke features or are specific client needs. Common components or part finished assemblies used with late customisation used.	**Hybrid Solution** Where there is a clear and predictable demand pattern, but solutions are bespoke, specially designed for the application, or customised to the clients specific requirements

Predictability and Stability of Demand

The Lean-Agile Matrix is used to understand the mix between adopting a Lean solution with a focus on: 1. maintaining a low or zero inventory; 2. manufacturing product to order, 3. versus having an Agile, flexible catalogue or product set which can be made quickly to a customer's specific requirements.

In addition, in some cases a compromise solution may be sought as in adopting a solution which relies on inventory (used where demand is erratic and/or there are long or unpredictable Supply Chains) or adopting close partnership solutions with consultants, architects, designers etc (often retained as an internal resource) which allow predictable demand for bespoke solutions to be produced in an efficient and timely fashion.

Positive Views on Model	Negative Views on Model
• Easy to understand four box model used to steer thinking • Identifies the core differences between concepts	• Suggests there is a clear two dimensional argument yet other factors have a clear influence

95. COUSINS STRATEGIC SUPPLY WHEEL

The Cousins Strategic Supply Wheel outlines six key factors that a Procurement and Supply professional faces and must consider individually and collectively when forming a corporate and supply relationship strategy.

The Strategic Supply Wheel stresses the importance of aligning corporate and procurement policies. A lack of connectivity makes it extremely difficult, if not impossible, for Procurement professionals to set their own polices, objectives and strategies whilst reflecting the needs, wants and direction of the organisation itself. The overall focus of the organisation, whether it is cost, quality or differentiation, will dictate the corporate and, therefore, procurement strategy.

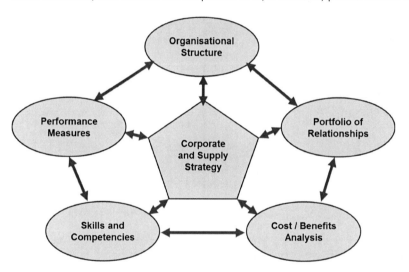

Procurement departments are typically given a high focus on cost reduction in organisations but should also have a major role in maintaining quality aspirations and on time delivery. Tactical methods of cost reduction with short to medium-term relationships are often favoured over more complex long-term relationships yet development of aspects such as measurement strategy, organisational structure and training all of which are key to success.

Positive Views on Model	Negative Views on Model
• Identifies core elements for attention and development within corporate strategy	• No reference to culture or the organisation's willingness to accept change

96. Enterprise Resource Planning Solutions (ERP)

Enterprise Resource Planning ERP solutions are IT packages designed to measure, manage and organise a Supply Chain from demand to delivery. Distribution Resource Planning (DRP) and Manufacturing Resource Planning (MRP) offer similar features for logistics and manufacturing activities.

ERP solutions are IT-related products produced by companies such as Manugistics, JDE, SAP, Oracle, etc. They are usually founded on a modular principle and allow the organisation to build an IT solution to manage the organisation's specific end–to–end Supply Chain (in the case of an ERP Solution).

This approach will ensure that the right quantity of quality resources – such as raw materials, utilities, personnel and finance – are available in the right place at the right time to provide the input necessary for the overall delivery requirements. The ERP solution will also have the option to interface with other facets of the organisation such as distribution, inventory management and accounting, amongst others.

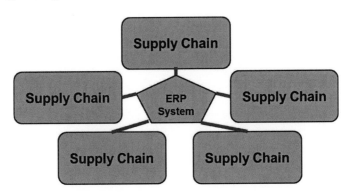

Modules within the system may include sales, procurement, inventory, logistics, warehousing, invoicing, goods receiving etc as required to help address all areas of the typical Supply Chain.

Positive Views on Model	Negative Views on Model
• Modular cross Supply Chain Solution • Flexible to reflect organisation activities and design	• Individual solutions may lack compatibility • May struggle to integrate to bespoke or historic systems

97. GOLDRATT THEORY OF CONSTRAINTS

The Goldratt Theory of Constraints concept suggests achievable goals may be set, yet constraints will always restrict achievement. Overcoming these constraints through continuous investigation and improvement is the secret to success.

The Goldratt Theory of Constraints was proposed by Goldratt in the late 1970s and suggested that an organisation would always be held back by its inability to overcome every constraint in its operating environment. Overcoming or addressing constraints would help the organisation achieve more of its goals, albeit that it may have to dramatically rethink or restructure its business operations to achieve this. Failure to address these constraints would mean that the organisation can never fulfil its true theoretical full potential, and whilst it has an issue – an "Achilles Heel" – it would always be vulnerable from hostile activity, uncertainty and risk.

To understand a constraint, the growth of value and throughput was examined. Paradoxically, growth cannot carry on to infinity therefore there must be a constraining factor at all times. As the goal of the organisation is usually to increase shareholder wealth, measurement of turnover and costs are key to this being achieved, both are finite concepts.

To overcome these constraints, the organisation needs to adopt a philosophy of continuous review, investigation and improvement, this Goldratt called the "Thinking Process" and follows five steps:

1. **Identify** what and where the constraint is;
2. **Assess** the constraint and decide on how to address it;
3. **Focus** on achieving these first two actions at the expense of others;
4. **Evaluate** the constraint and monitor it in an operational context;
5. **Repeat** if the constraint is overcome with the new constraint that replaces the first.

Positive Views on Model	Negative Views on Model
• Useful model in manufacturing and project scenarios • Needs clarity of goals to help focus on the constraints	• Perceived by some as being unduly pessimistic • Competition used by some Not–For–Profit groups instead of constraining theories

98. Incoterms

Incoterms are an established and internationally recognised method of identifying the responsibilities for shipping and insurance liability. They are used to indicate the moment at which ownership switches between seller and buyer and can be used to ensure the reciprocal release of funds or value at a given time using letter of credit or similar mechanisms.

Incoterms are the primary mechanism or tool used in international trade (and indeed intra–national logistics) for knowing who is responsible for what and when. They cover the point of handover, the responsibility for costs of insurance and logistics, as well as liability for any issues caused including accidents and environmental issues such as pollution. They are invariably used in legal contracts, shipping directives, and negotiations.

Different Incoterms are available at any given time, and are reviewed periodically and amended to reflect any changes in circumstances and the prevailing situations. Some of these are shown in the diagram below at various points between the despatch gate of the Supplier (Ex-Works) and delivery at the Buyer's premises with all taxes and levies paid (Delivery Duty Paid).

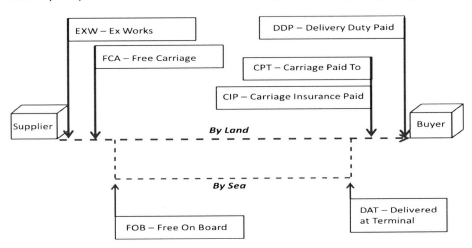

Positive Views on Model	Negative Views on Model
• Internationally recognised • Functionally easy to understand and apply	• Incoterms change with education and contracts not reflecting the changes

99. Jackson Inventory Decision Matrix

The Inventory Decision Matrix is a four box model which assesses the inventory decision process based on two core factors affecting inventory; the impact of a stock–out and the ease and speed with which the product can be sourced in the market. The model goes on to highlight ways to reduce inventory through addressing the impact and sourcing issues.

The Inventory Decision Model considers inventory decisions based on two dimensions – the impact on the organisation of a stock-out versus the ease with which the item can be obtained in the market – and promotes strategy to reduce impact and improve the ease of sourcing. These two dimensions combine to steer the stock decision-making process.

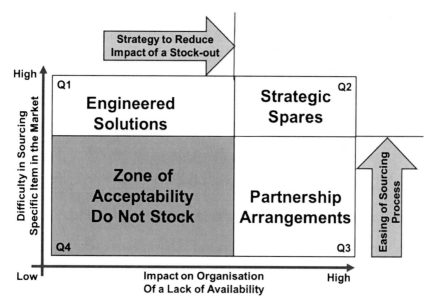

Once the core observations of the Inventory Decision Matrix have been implemented as directed by the four box directives, the longer term effort should be to draw dependent and independent demand into the bottom left quadrant with strategies to reduce the impact of a stock out and overcoming the sourcing obstacles.

Positive Views on Model	Negative Views on Model
• Addresses the core drivers of inventory	• Dependent and independent inventory treated as one

100. Outsourcing Decision Model

The Outsourcing Decision Model looks at the options available when an organisation is contemplating outsourcing a process or service. It considers two variables, namely the risk exposure of the supplier capability and the risk exposure of the client capability.

A process/service should be outsourced when the risk exposure of a supplier capability to deliver the service is lower than, or equal to that of the buying organisation. The model highlights the relationship between the risk exposure of the two parties.

In quadrant 1, risk exposure of the Supplier capability is low, and that of the Client is high, so it will be prudent to *outsource*. Outsourcing is also a valid option when both parties have low risk as in quadrant 2, although in this instance, the client should *outsource* to enable it to focus on aspects which it is good at an generate a more favourable return. When the risk exposure of the client is low and the supplier's high, then *in-house* is optimal as in quadrant 4. In some situations when both have high risk, it may be prudent to develop *capabilities in-house* whilst supporting suppliers to *develop capabilities* as in quadrant 3.

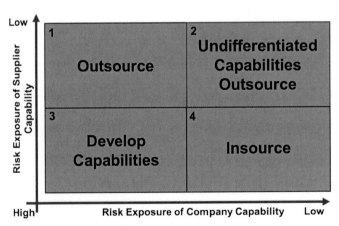

The effectiveness of this model is predicated by the ability of the Client to effectively assess the relative risks accurately. However, it does focus the mind in terms of risk assessment of *outsourcing*.

Bhattachchary et al 2003

Positive Views on Model	Negative Views on Model
• Gives clear direction based on the corporate risk profile	• Doesn't consider market trends, resource availability, etc • Duplicates Greaver (1999)

101. PORTER VALUE CHAIN

The Porter Value Chain can be used to identify where in an organisation's business activities it generates value. The Value Chain splits the organisation into Primary and Secondary business facets enabling the analyst to evaluate more precisely the value contribution of each element.

The Porter Value Chain (1985) segments the organisation's operational activities into *Primary* and *Secondary* operations allowing the value attained from each to be quantified and understood.

The value can be evaluated in various ways – financial contribution, time saved, quality improved, etc. – and strategy can be adopted to improve the value generated in each. It is common to use this model in conjunction with others, for example a SWOT/TOWS analysis to enable tangible outcomes and deliverables to be established.

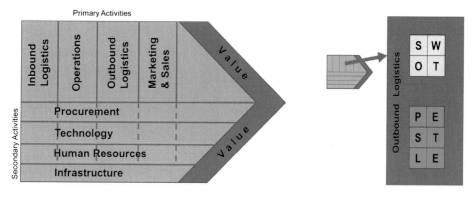

The model also recognises that some functions such as Procurement or HR transcend the organisation, adding specific value, and highlight that a unified and consistent strategy helps add value here also allowing critical points in an organisation's business activities to be identified.

Positive Views on Model	Negative Views on Model
• Long–established model • Can be adapted to include numbers and magnitude	• Understanding of the model often poor and can be difficult to populate with numbers • Product not service orientated

Conclusion

Throughout this book we have endeavoured to highlight some of the most popular models in modern Procurement and Supply Chain Management in such a way as to make sense of them for the student studying for exams and useful for the practitioner in his or her work.

Many of the models are intended to generate thought or collate ideas, some generate meaningful output in their own right, whilst others are merely used to communicate or illustrate an idea, concept or strategy.

This book has intended to decipher the mystique, bestow the virtues and highlight the pitfalls of academic theories and models so that the reader can decide which, if any, they will use in their exams or their work.

Whether transmitting a message within or outside the organisation, communication skills will be of paramount importance, in many instances shaping, making or breaking the message. Models need to be incorporated into an effective communication strategy, imbedded in a wider proposal or used to underpin a point in an exam or thesis. Use of effective communication methods is therefore often as important as the message itself, as is the use of graphs, images, and other graphics to illustrate a point, see below.

When transmitting this message, think outside the box; use innovative graphics as above, or English literacy techniques such as Onomatopoeia, Alliteration, Assonance and Metaphors, or techniques from the great orators of history.

Furthermore, think about simplistic messages. As detailed in the Jackson POINT model (see Model 44) a human mind cannot take in and remember complicated images or text, there is the Power of Three concept that suggests you should never use more than three colours, three types, sizes, or styles of text as this will overload the brain and the message will be diminished; Politicians use this when speaking often giving three reasons for something, and often use techniques such as PREP (Point–Reason–Example–Point) when speaking to make a Point, explain it, give credibility with an example, before reiterating the Point.

Life and business is far from simplistic, these models help to unravel and explain the concepts and theories of business.

And remember, in exams, "Models Mean Marks".

Appendix 1 // Model by Business Facet

Model Number	Model	Quality	Cost	Time	Value	Risk	Stakeholders	Strategy	Contract Mgt	Procurement	Relationships	HR Management	Market Analysis	Environment	Waste
1	Burnes & New Customer/Supplier Relationships			✓							✓	✓			
2	Cox Supplier Relationships Management Model							✓			✓	✓			
3	Crocker Managing Satisfaction of Service Quality Model							✓			✓	✓			
4	Customer-Supplier Partnership Bridge							✓			✓	✓			
5	Purchaser-Supplier Satisfaction Model							✓			✓	✓			
6	Relationship Determination Model							✓			✓	✓			
7	Supplier Relationship Management (SRM) Interfaces							✓			✓	✓			
8	Watson & Sanderson Buyer-Supplier Power Model							✓			✓	✓			
9	Carter 6S Contract Management Model	✓	✓				✓	✓	✓	✓	✓				✓
10	Jackson SPARKLE Model				✓	✓	✓	✓	✓		✓			✓	✓
11	Kotler 8 Phases of Change							✓	✓		✓				
12	Lewin Freeze Model							✓	✓		✓				
13	Carter STOPWASTE Model	✓	✓	✓			✓	✓	✓	✓					✓
14	Eight R Model of Responsible Waste Treatment				✓	✓		✓						✓	✓
15	Jackson Sustainability Impact Model		✓	✓									✓	✓	✓
16	Jackson Nine Dimensions of Sustainability		✓		✓		✓						✓	✓	✓
17	Three E Model							✓						✓	✓
18	Ansoff Planning Model	✓	✓	✓	✓	✓	✓	✓	✓	✓					✓
19	Ashridge Management Styles							✓	✓			✓			
20	Balanced Scorecards	✓	✓	✓	✓			✓	✓						✓
21	Critical Needs Analysis (CNA)	✓		✓	✓		✓								
22	Fayol Principles of Management								✓			✓			
23	Greiner Growth Model						✓	✓	✓			✓			
24	Hersey-Blanchard Model							✓				✓			
25	Hierarchy of Objectives						✓	✓	✓			✓			
26	Jackson Fraud and Corruption Plan		✓			✓	✓	✓		✓	✓	✓			
27	Johnson Supplier Management Behaviours Model		✓				✓	✓		✓	✓				
28	McKinsey 7S Model	✓	✓	✓		✓		✓				✓			✓
29	Mintzberg 5P Model	✓	✓	✓				✓	✓				✓	✓	
30	Pareto Analysis		✓	✓		✓		✓							
31	PEST / PESTLE / STEEPLE / STEEPLED Analysis	✓	✓	✓	✓	✓	✓	✓	✓				✓	✓	✓
32	RACI Assessment		✓				✓	✓	✓		✓				
33	Rogers Seven Point Plan							✓			✓	✓			
34	Senge Five Disciplines						✓	✓			✓	✓			
35	SMART Objectives						✓	✓	✓		✓	✓			
36	SWOT Analysis & TOWS Strategy Model						✓	✓	✓		✓	✓			
37	Adair Action-Centred Leadership Model							✓			✓	✓			
38	Adizes Management Profiles						✓	✓	✓		✓	✓			
39	Belbin Team Roles						✓	✓			✓	✓			
40	Crocker Triangle	✓	✓	✓				✓	✓		✓	✓			
41	Handy Organisational Culture Model						✓	✓			✓	✓			
42	Herzberg Hygiene/Motivators	✓	✓	✓	✓	✓	✓	✓			✓	✓			
43	Hofstede Cultural Factors Model						✓	✓			✓	✓			
44	Jackson POINT Model							✓			✓	✓			
45	Jackson RITUAL							✓			✓	✓			
46	Johnson Cultural Web							✓	✓		✓	✓			
47	Lewin Force Field Analysis						✓	✓			✓	✓			
48	Maslow Hierarchy of Needs							✓			✓	✓			
49	Mintzberg Management Roles						✓	✓	✓		✓	✓			
50	Theory X, Theory Y and Theory Z						✓	✓	✓		✓	✓			
51	Tuckman Team Development Cycle						✓	✓	✓		✓	✓			
52	Porter Competitive Advantage Model	✓	✓	✓	✓	✓		✓		✓			✓		
53	Porter Five Force Model	✓	✓	✓	✓	✓		✓		✓			✓		
54	Pricing Strategies	✓	✓	✓	✓	✓		✓					✓		
55	Supply Market Analysis	✓	✓	✓	✓	✓		✓		✓			✓		
56	Ansoff Matrix	✓	✓	✓	✓	✓		✓		✓			✓		

#	Model													
57	Boston Consulting Group Matrix	✓	✓	✓	✓	✓		✓					✓	
58	Kotler 4P Model	✓	✓	✓	✓	✓		✓					✓	
59	Product Life Cycle	✓	✓	✓	✓	✓		✓					✓	
60	Activity Based Costing	✓	✓	✓			✓	✓	✓	✓				
61	Bartolini Scorecard	✓	✓	✓	✓	✓	✓	✓		✓	✓			
62	Carter 9C Model	✓	✓	✓	✓	✓	✓	✓	✓	✓			✓	✓
63	Crocker Simplified Service Gap Model	✓	✓	✓		✓	✓	✓	✓		✓			
64	Five Rights of Purchasing	✓	✓	✓	✓	✓	✓			✓				
65	Kraljic Matrix	✓	✓	✓	✓	✓	✓	✓		✓	✓			
66	Maturity Assessment Model						✓	✓		✓		✓		
67	Monczka MSU Model	✓	✓	✓	✓	✓	✓	✓		✓				
68	O'Brien 5i Model	✓	✓	✓	✓	✓				✓				
69	POD Procurement Model			✓	✓		✓	✓	✓	✓	✓			
70	Steele & Court Supplier Preferencing Model	✓	✓		✓	✓	✓	✓		✓	✓			
71	Syson Positioning Graph - Strategic Policies	✓	✓	✓	✓	✓	✓	✓		✓				
71a	Syson Positioning Graph - Strategic Perfromance	✓	✓	✓	✓	✓	✓	✓		✓				
72	Total Cost of Ownership Model	✓	✓	✓	✓	✓	✓	✓		✓				
73	Value Analysis & Value Stream Mapping	✓	✓	✓	✓	✓	✓	✓		✓				
74	5 Whys	✓	✓	✓	✓	✓	✓		✓					
75	Cost of Poor Quality (COPQ) Model	✓	✓	✓	✓	✓	✓		✓					
76	Deming / Shewhart Plan-Do-Check-Act (PDCA)	✓	✓	✓	✓	✓	✓		✓					
77	EFQM Excellence Model	✓	✓	✓	✓	✓	✓		✓	✓		✓		
78	Fishbone / Root Cause Analysis / Ishikawa Diagram	✓	✓	✓	✓	✓	✓		✓					
79	Iron Triangle Model	✓	✓	✓	✓	✓	✓		✓	✓				
80	Kaizen	✓	✓	✓	✓	✓	✓		✓					
81	Ohno Seven Wastes	✓	✓	✓	✓	✓	✓		✓	✓				
82	Quality Circles	✓	✓	✓	✓	✓	✓		✓		✓			
83	Six Sigma, DMAIC and SIPOC Models	✓	✓	✓	✓	✓	✓		✓		✓			
84	Toyota 3M Model	✓	✓	✓	✓	✓	✓		✓		✓			
85	Voice of the Customer	✓	✓	✓	✓	✓	✓			✓	✓			
86	Four T Model of Risk	✓	✓	✓	✓	✓		✓	✓					
87	Risk-Impact Model	✓	✓	✓	✓	✓		✓	✓					
88	Risk Types					✓		✓	✓					
89	The Risk Cycle	✓	✓	✓	✓	✓		✓	✓					
90	Egan Stakeholder Positioning Model						✓			✓	✓			
91	Mendelow Matrix						✓			✓	✓			
92	Stakeholder Allegiance Matrix						✓			✓	✓			
93	Stakeholder Attitudes Model						✓			✓	✓			
94	Christopher & Towill Lean Agile Matrix	✓	✓	✓	✓	✓	✓	✓	✓	✓	✓			
95	Cousins Strategic Supply Wheel	✓	✓	✓	✓	✓		✓	✓	✓	✓			
96	Enterprise Resource Planning Solutions (ERP)	✓	✓	✓	✓	✓	✓	✓	✓	✓				
97	Goldratt Theory of Constraints		✓	✓		✓		✓	✓		✓			
98	Incoterms	✓	✓	✓		✓		✓	✓	✓			✓	
99	Jackson Inventory Decision Matrix	✓	✓	✓	✓	✓	✓	✓	✓	✓	✓			
100	Outsourcing Decision Model	✓	✓	✓	✓	✓	✓	✓	✓	✓	✓		✓	
101	Porter Value Chain	✓	✓	✓	✓		✓	✓	✓	✓				

BIBLIOGRAPHY

Adizes, I. (1979). *How to Solve the Mismanagement Crisis.* The Adizes Institute.

Obeng, E. (1995). *All Change! The Project Leader's Secret Handbook.* FT Press.

Chan Kim, W. & Mauborgne, R. (2005). *Blue Ocean Strategy.* Harvard Business Review Press.

Tang, K. (ed). (2007). *Cut Carbon Grow Profit: Business Strategies for Managing Climate Change and Sustainability (Management, Policy + Education).* Libri Publishing.

Kaplan, R.S. & Norton, D.P. (1992). *Essentials of Balanced Scorecards.* Harvard Business Review Press.

Emmett, S. & Crocker, B. (2010). *Excellence in Global Supply Chain Management.* Cambridge: Cambridge Academic.

Emmett, S. & Crocker, B. (2013) *Excellence in Procurement Strategy.* Cambridge: Cambridge Academic.

Emmett, S., Crocker, B. & Moore, D. (2010). *Excellence in Services Procurement.* Cambridge: Cambridge Academic.

Emmett, S. & Crocker, B. (2009). *Excellence in Supplier Management.* Cambridge: Cambridge Academic.

Kreps, D. (1990). *Game Theory and Economic Modelling.* Clarendon Press.

Turner, R. (2008). *Gower Handbook of Project Management.* Ashgate.

Emmett, S. & Sood, V. (2010). *Green Supply Chains.* Wiley.

Cox, A. (2003). 'Horses for Courses', *Supply Management* (30 January 2003) 28-29.

Syson, R. (1992). *Improving Purchase Performance.* Financial Times Prentice Hall.

Carter, R. & Price, P. (1998). *Integrated Material Management.* Financial Times Prentice Hall.

Beckman, R. (1988). *Into the Upwave: How to Prosper from Slump to Boom.* Milestone Publications.

Lamming, R. (1996). *Lean Procurement & Global Sourcing.* Prentice Hall.

Womack, J. & Jones, D. (1996). *Lean Thinking: Banish Waste and Create Wealth in Your Corporation.* Productivity Press.

Pearn, M., Roderick, C. & Mulrooney, C. (1995). *Learning Organisations in Practice.* Mcgraw Hill Book Co Ltd.

Eden, C. and Ackermann, F. (1998). *Making Strategy: The Journey of Strategic Management.* London: SAGE Publications.

Kotler, P & Renshaw, G. (1994). *Marketing Management.* Prentice Hall.

Buchanon, D. & Huczynski, A. (2004). *Organisational Behaviour.* Financial Times Management.

Cook, M. (1998). *Outsourcing Human Resources Functions.* AMACOM.

Cox, A., Sanderson, J., Watson, G. & Lonsdale, C. (1997). *Power Regimes: A Strategic Perspective on the Management of Business-to-Business Relationships in Supply Networks.* Financial Times Prentice Hall.

Carter, R. & Kirby, S. (2006). *Practical Procurement.* Cambridge: Cambridge Academic.

Bailey, P., Farmer, D., Crocker, B., Jessop, D. & Jones, D. (2008). *Procurement, Principles and Management.* Prentice Hall.

Williams, B. (2005). *Six Sigma for Managers.* Wiley.

Carter, R., Price R., & Emmett, S. (2004). *Stores Distribution & Management.* Cambridge: Cambridge Academic.

Bryson, J. (1995). *Strategic Planning for Public and Nonprofit Organizations: A Guide to Strengthening and Sustaining Organizational Achievement.* Jossey-Bass.

Cousins, P., Lamming, R., Lawson, B. and Squire, B., 2008. Strategic Supply Management:Principles, Theories and Practice. Pearson Education.

Harvard Business School. (2005). *Strategy Harvard Business Essentials.*

Bolstroff, P. (2007). *Supply Chain Excellence.* AMACOM.

Cox, A. & Ireland, P. (2001). *Supply Chains, Markets and Power: Managing Buyer and Supplier Power Regimes.* Routledge.

Goldsmith, Z. (1988). *The Constant Economy.* London: Atlantic Books.

Zahhly, J. & Tosi, H. (1989). 'The differential effect of organizational induction process on early work role adjustment' in *The Journal of Organisational Behaviour.* Volume 10 (1) – Jan 1, 1989.

Alexander, M. (2001). *The Kondratiev Cycle and Secular Market Trends.* Writers Club.

Womack, J., Jones, D. & Roos, D. (1990). *The Machine That Changed the World: The Story of Lean Production – Toyota's Secret Weapon in the Global Car Wars That Is Now Revolutionizing World Industry.* Free Press.

Emmett, S., & Crocker B. (2009) *The Relationship Driven Supply Chain.* Gower Publishing.

Pyzdek, T. & Keller, P. (2008). *The Six Sigma Handbook.* McGraw-Hill Education.

Smith, J.H. (2000). *The Wiremold Company: A century of solutions.* Greenwich Pub. Group.

Pearn, M. & Mulrooney, C. (2003). *Tools for the Learning Organisation.* Mcgraw Hill Book Co Ltd.

Lawler, E.E. & Lawler, C.O. (2011). *Treat People Right*. Jossey-Bass.

Selected excerpts, citations and references from:
Profex (CIPS) Study Guides
CIPS Technical publications
Institute of Director's publications
Institute of Mechanical Engineer's publications
National Geographic
Supplier Management
The Economist
International Marine Purchasing Association Periodical
The Financial Times & Supplements
Time

INDEX